THE SPEECH

THE SPEECH

The Story behind
Dr. Martin Luther King Jr.'s Dream

GARY YOUNGE

Haymarket Books
Chicago, Illinois

Published in 2013 by
Haymarket Books
P.O. Box 180165,
Chicago, IL 60618
773-583-7884
info@haymarketbooks.org
www.haymarketbooks.org

ISBN: 978-1-60846-322-0

Trade distribution in the United States through Consortium Book Sales
and Distribution, www.cbsd.com

Text of Dr. Martin Luther King Jr.'s "I Have a Dream" speech reprinted by
arrangement with The Heirs to the Estate of Martin Luther King Jr., c/o
Writers House as agent for the proprietor, New York, NY.

Cover design by Abby Weintraub. Cover image of Dr. Martin Luther King
Jr. speaking at the March on Washington for Jobs and Freedom, August 28,
1963. US Information Agency.

This book was published with the generous support of the Wallace Global
Fund and Lannan Foundation.

Printed in Canada by union labor.

Library of Congress CIP data is available.

10 9 8 7 6 5 4 3 2 1

Contents

Acknowledgments

THIS BOOK STEMS from my long-standing interest in the American South and commitment to issues of social justice. The two came together, not for the first time, in 2011 when I conducted two public interviews, in London and Glasgow, with Clarence Jones, who wrote the draft text of Martin Luther King's speech at the March on Washington. I have long been intrigued by how the speech became lionized and the wildly conflicting interpretations of it that have circulated. And my conversations with Jones, both on and off stage, showed me that the manner in which the speech was written and delivered, the political moment that made it possible, and the occasion at which it was given said as much about the speech as the words themselves.

This book includes many interviews I have conducted over the last sixteen years with a range of civil rights leaders, activists, and other political and cultural commentators. To present a full and vivid portrayal, it also weaves together a number of other autobiographical and historical accounts of which I am not the source. All are listed in the bibliography and credited frequently throughout the book. But in the absence of footnotes and out of respect for their contributions, I would also like to express a particular debt of gratitude to the hard work and scholarship of a few without whom this book would not have been possible: Drew Hansen, author of *The Dream: Martin Luther King Jr. and the Speech That Inspired a Nation*; Charles Euchner, who wrote *Nobody Turn Me Around: A People's History of the 1963 March on Washington*; Nick Bryant, author of *The Bystander: John F. Kennedy and The Struggle for Black Equality*; and Taylor Branch for *Parting the Waters: America in the King Years, 1954–63*. These books were not just invaluable to my research, they are invaluable, period.

Also crucial to this book and the body of work focusing on this era are *Eyes on The Prize* by Juan Williams, *The Life and Times of Bayard Rustin* by John D'Emilio, and *My Soul Is Rested* by Howell Raines, as well as the accounts of Clarence Jones in *Behind the Dream* and John Lewis in *Walking with the Wind*.

I'd also like to thank Julie Fain, my Haymarket editor, for immediately realizing the potential for this book and supporting me throughout its writing; Anthony Arnove, also of Haymarket, for his lucid and consistent advice and encouragement; Ruth Goring, whose precision and clarity made substantial improvements; and the staff at Haymarket who've worked so hard to promote the book within a tight schedule. In his editing of the first draft, Colin Robinson's speed and attention to detail went above and beyond the call of duty. I thank my agent, Jonny Geller, for more than a decade of advocating for my work and representing my interests on both sides of the Atlantic.

Finally, I'd like to thank Tara and Osceola for bearing with me as I wrote it, and Zora, who came into this world right in the middle of it.

"I Have a Dream"

Address delivered at the March on Washington for Jobs and Freedom

AUGUST 28, 1963
WASHINGTON, DC

I AM HAPPY TO JOIN WITH YOU TODAY on what will go down in history as the greatest demonstration for freedom in the history of our nation. [*applause*]

Fivescore years ago, a great American, in whose symbolic shadow we stand today, signed the Emancipation Proclamation. This momentous decree came as a great beacon light of hope to millions of Negro slaves who had been seared in the flames of withering injustice. It came as a joyous daybreak to end the long night of their captivity.

But one hundred years later, the Negro still is not free. [*Audience:*] (*My Lord*) One hundred years later, the life of the Negro is still sadly crippled by the manacles of segregation and the chains of discrimination. One hundred years later, the Negro lives on a lonely island of poverty in the midst of a vast ocean of material prosperity. One hundred years later (*My Lord*) [*applause*], the Negro is still languished in the corners of American society and finds himself an exile in his own land. And so we've come here today to dramatize a shameful condition.

In a sense we've come to our nation's capital to cash a check. When the architects of our Republic wrote the magnificent words of the Constitution and the Declaration of Independence (*Yeah*), they were signing a promissory note to which every American was to fall heir. This note was a promise that all men, yes, black men as well as white men, would be guaranteed the "unalienable Rights" of "Life, Liberty, and the pursuit of Happiness." It is obvious today that America has defaulted on this promissory note insofar as her citizens of colors are concerned. Instead of honoring this sacred obligation, America has given the Negro people a bad check, a check which has come back marked "insufficient funds." [*sustained applause*]

But we refuse to believe that the bank of justice is bankrupt. (*My Lord*) [*laughter*] (*Sure enough*) We refuse to believe that there are insufficient funds in the great vaults of opportunity of this nation. And so we've come to cash this check (*Yes*), a check that will give us upon demand the riches of freedom (*Yes*) and the security of justice. [*applause*]

We have also come to this hallowed spot to remind America of the fierce urgency of now. This is no time (*My Lord*) to engage in the luxury of cooling off or to take the tranquilizing drug of gradualism. [*applause*] Now is the time to make real the promises of democracy. (*My Lord*) Now is the time to rise from the dark and desolate valley of segregation to the sunlit path of racial justice. Now is the time [*applause*] to lift our nation from the quicksand of racial injustice to the solid rock of brotherhood. Now is the time [*applause*] to make justice a reality for all of God's children.

It would be fatal for the nation to overlook the urgency of the moment. This sweltering summer of the Negro's legitimate discontent will not pass until there is an invigorating autumn of freedom and equality. Nineteen sixty-three is not an end, but a beginning. And those who hope that the Negro needed to blow off steam and will now be content will have a rude awakening if the nation returns to business as usual. [*applause*] There will be neither rest nor tranquility in America until the Negro is granted his citizenship rights. The whirlwinds of revolt will continue to shake the foundations of our nation until the bright day of justice emerges.

But there is something that I must say to my people, who stand on the warm threshold which leads into the palace of justice: In the process of gaining our rightful place, we must not be guilty of wrongful deeds. Let us not seek to satisfy our thirst for freedom by drinking from the cup of bitterness and hatred. (*My Lord*) [*applause*] We must forever conduct our struggle on the high place of dignity and discipline. We must not allow our creative protest to degenerate into physical violence. Again and again, we must rise to the majestic heights of meeting physical force with soul force. The marvelous new militancy which has engulfed the Negro community must not lead us to a distrust of all white people, for many of our white brothers, as evidenced by their presence here today, have come to realize that their destiny is tied up with our destiny. [*applause*] And they have come to realize that their freedom is inextricably bound to our freedom. We cannot walk alone.

And as we walk, we must make the pledge that we shall always march ahead. We cannot turn back. There are those who are asking the devotees of civil rights, "When will you be satisfied?" (*Never*)

We can never be satisfied as long as the Negro is the victim of the unspeakable horrors of police brutality. We can never be satisfied [*applause*] as long as our bodies, heavy with the fatigue of travel, cannot gain lodging in the motels of the highways and the hotels of the cities. [*applause*] We cannot be satisfied as long as the Negro's basic mobility is from a smaller ghetto to a larger one. We can never be satisfied as long as our children are stripped of their selfhood and robbed of their dignity by signs stating: "For Whites Only." [*applause*] We cannot be satisfied as long as a Negro in Mississippi cannot vote and a Negro in New York believes he has nothing for which to vote. (*Yes*) [*applause*] No, no, we are not satisfied and we will not be satisfied until "justice rolls down like waters and righteousness like a mighty stream." [*applause*]

I am not unmindful that some of you have come here out of great trials and tribulations. (*My Lord*) Some of you have come fresh from narrow jail cells. Some of you have come from areas where your quest for freedom left you battered by the storms of persecution (*Yes*) and staggered by the winds of police brutality. You have been veterans of creative suffering. Continue to work with the faith that unearned suffering is redemptive. Go back to Mississippi (*Yes*), go back to Alabama, go back to South Carolina, go back to Georgia, go back to Louisiana, go back to the slums and ghettos of our northern cities, knowing that somehow this situation can and will be changed. (*Yes*) Let us not wallow in the valley of despair, I say to you today, my friends [*applause*].

And so even though we face the difficulties of today and tomorrow, I still have a dream. (*Yes*) It is a dream deeply rooted in the American dream.

I have a dream that one day (*Yes*) this nation will rise up and live out the true meaning of its creed: "We hold these truths to be self-evident, that all men are created equal." (*Yes*) [*applause*]

I have a dream that one day on the red hills of Georgia, the sons of former slaves and the sons of former slave owners will be able to sit down together at the table of brotherhood.

I have a dream that one day even the state of Mississippi, a state sweltering with the heat of injustice (*Well*), sweltering with the heat of oppression, will be transformed into an oasis of freedom and justice.

I have a dream (*Well*) [*applause*] that my four little children will one day live in a nation where they will not be judged by the color of their skin but by the content of their character. (*My Lord*) I have a dream today. [*applause*]

I have a dream that one day down in Alabama, with its vicious racists, with its governor having his lips dripping with the words of "interposition" and "nullification," (*Yes*) one day right there in Alabama little black boys and black girls will be able to join hands with little white boys and white girls as sisters and brothers. I have a dream today. [*applause*]

I have a dream that one day "every valley shall be exalted (*Yes*), and every hill and mountain shall be made low; the rough places will be made plain, and the crooked places will be made straight (*Yes*); and the glory of the Lord shall be revealed, and all flesh shall see it together." (*Yes*)

This is our hope. This is the faith that I go back to the South with. (*Yes*) With this faith we will be able to hew out of the mountain of despair a stone of hope. (*Yes*) With this faith we will be able to transform the jangling discords of our nation into a beautiful symphony of brotherhood. (*talk about it*) With this faith (*My Lord*) we will be able to work together, to pray together, to struggle together, to go to jail together, to stand up for freedom together, knowing that we will be free one day. [*applause*] And this will be the day [*applause continues*], this will be the day when all of God's children (*Yes*) will be able to sing with new meaning

> *My country, 'tis of thee (Yes), sweet land of liberty, of thee I sing*
> *Land where my fathers dies, land of the pilgrim's pride (Yes),*
> *From every mountainside, let freedom ring!*

And if America is to be a great nation, this must become true.

And so let freedom ring (*Yes*) from the prodigious hilltops of New Hampshire.

Let freedom ring from the mighty mountains of New York.

Let freedom ring from the heightening Alleghenies of Pennsylvania. (*Yes, that's right*)

Let freedom ring from the snow-capped Rockies of Colorado. (*Well*)

Let freedom ring from the curvaceous slopes of California. (*Yes*)

But not only that: Let freedom ring from Stone Mountain of Georgia. (*Yes*)

Let freedom ring from Lookout Mountain of Tennessee. (*Yes*)

Let freedom ring from every hill and molehill of Mississippi. (*Yes*)

From every mountainside, let freedom ring. [*applause*]

And when this happens [*applause continues*], when we allow freedom to ring, when we let it ring from every village and every hamlet, from every state and every city (*Yes*), we will be able to speed up that day when all of God's children, black men and white men, Jews and Gentiles, Protestants and Catholics, will be able to join hands and sing in the words of the old Negro spiritual:

> *Free at last! (Yes) Free at last!*
> *Thank God Almighty, we are free at last!* [applause]

Introduction
Lightning in a Bottle

THE NIGHT BEFORE THE MARCH on Washington in 1963, Martin Luther King Jr. asked his aides for advice about the speech he was due to make the next day. "Don't use the lines about 'I have a dream,'" Wyatt Tee Walker told him. "It's trite, it's cliché. You've used it too many times already."

King had indeed employed the refrain several times before. It had featured in an address just a week earlier at a National Insurance Association fundraiser in Chicago and a few months before that at a huge rally in Detroit. Like most of his speeches, both had been well received. But neither had been regarded as particularly momentous.

While King, by this time, was a national political figure, relatively few outside the Black church and the civil rights movement had heard him give a full speech. With all three television networks offering live coverage of the March for Jobs and Freedom (the biggest event of its kind in the country's history), this would be his introduction to the nation. He wanted a speech to fit the occasion.

Sitting in the lobby of Washington's Willard Hotel, King called on his team for ideas. Walker's was one contribution of many. "Suggestions just tumbled out," recalled Clarence Jones, who wrote the final draft. "'I think you should . . .' 'Why don't we . . .' 'Martin, as I mentioned before . . .'"

After a few hours King thanked them for their input. "I am now going upstairs to my room to counsel with my Lord," he said. "I will see you all tomorrow." When one of his advisers went to his room later that night, he had crossed out some words three or four times. King went to sleep at around 4 a.m.

A few hours later the march's organizer, Bayard Rustin, wandered onto the Mall with some of his assistants to find security personnel and journalists outnumbering demonstrators. That morning a television news reporter in DC announced: "Not many people seem to be showing up. It doesn't look as if it's going to be very much." The movement had high hopes for a large turnout and had originally set a goal of 100,000. From the reservations on coaches and trains alone, they guessed they should be at least close to that figure. But when the actual morning came, that did little to calm their nerves. Reporters badgered Rustin about the ramifications for both the event and the movement if the crowd turned out to be smaller than anticipated. Rustin, forever theatrical, took a round pocket watch from his trousers and some paper from his jacket. Examining first the paper and then the watch, he turned to the reporters and said: "Everything is right on schedule." The piece of paper was blank.

As the morning progressed, the organizers' apprehension subsided as the capital was transformed by protesters flooding in from all over the country. The first official Freedom Train arrived at Washington's Union Station from Pittsburgh at 8:02, records Charles Euchner in *Nobody Turn Me Around: A People's History of the 1963 March on Washington*. Soon trains were pulling in every five to ten minutes. At the height of the flow, ten thousand people came through the station in twenty minutes while one hundred buses an hour rolled through the Baltimore Harbor Tunnel. By 10 a.m. the magnitude of the march was beyond doubt.

"We were surrounded by a moving sea of humanity," wrote John Lewis, a young civil rights leader who addressed the crowd that day, as the throng began to move. "Tens of thousands of people just pouring out of Union Station, filling Constitution Avenue from curb to curb. It was truly awesome, the most incredible thing I'd ever seen in my life. I remember thinking, There goes *America*."

Singers, including Joan Baez, Bob Dylan, Josh White, Odetta, and Peter, Paul and Mary kept the crowds entertained. Marchers who brought their own placards made a wide variety of demands and statements. "Horses have their own television shows. Dogs have their own television shows. Why Can't Negroes have their own shows?" read one. "No US Dough to help Jim Crow Grow," announced another. Yet another read: "Our Body in Motion, Our Life on the Line, We Demand Freedom of Mind."

◆

RUSTIN HAD LIMITED THE SPEAKERS that day to just five minutes each and threatened to come on with a crook and haul them from the podium when their time was up. But they all overran, and given the heat—87 degrees at noon—and the humidity, the mood began to wane.

"There was . . . an air of subtle depression, of wistful apathy which existed in many," wrote Norman Mailer. "One felt a little of the muted disappointment which attacks a crowd in the seventh inning of a very important baseball game when the score has gone 11-3. The home team is ahead, but the tension is broken: one's concern is no longer noble."

King was the last speaker. By the time he reached the podium, many in the crowd had started to leave. "I tell students today, 'There were no Jumbotrons back then,'" Rachelle Horowitz, who as a young activist had organized transport to the march, told me. "All people could see was a speck and they listened to it." Not all those who remained could hear him properly, but those who could stood rapt. "Go back to Mississippi, go back to Alabama, go back to South Carolina, go back to Georgia, go back to Louisiana, go back to the slums and ghettos of our northern cities, knowing that somehow this situation can and will be changed," said King as though he were wrapping up. "Let us not wallow in the valley of despair, I say to you today, my friends."

Then he grabbed the podium and set his prepared text to his left. "When he was reading from his text, he stood like a lecturer," Jones told me. "But from the moment he set that text aside, he took on the stance of a Baptist preacher." Jones turned to the person standing next to him and said: "Those people don't know it but they're about to go to church."

A smattering of applause filled a pause more pregnant than most.

"So even though we face the difficulties of today and tomorrow, I still have a dream."

"Aw shit," said Wyatt Walker, who was on the Mall. "He's using the dream."

✦

WHILE THE OVERALL RESPONSE to the speech was favorable at the time, reviews were mixed. The *New York Times* ran a front page story with the headline "I Have a Dream"; the *Washington Post* editorial didn't refer to the "I have a dream" passage at all. The *Clarion-Ledger* in Jackson, Mississippi, ran a front-page photograph of the litter left behind with the headline: "Washington Is Clean Again with Negro Trash Removed."

Anne Moody, a Black activist who'd made the trip from rural Mississippi, recalled: "I sat on the grass and listened to the speakers, to discover we had 'dreamers' instead of leaders leading us. Just about every one of them stood up there dreaming. Martin Luther King went on and on talking about his dream. I sat there thinking that in Canton we never had time to sleep, much less dream." The late Edward Kennedy called it "the great aria of the civil rights movement." Malcolm X told Rustin: "You know, this dream of King's is going to be a nightmare before it's over." Motown set it in vinyl. John Lewis wrote in his autobiography, *Walking with the Wind*: "Despite its lack of substance . . . more than anyone else that summer afternoon in 1963, [King] captured the spirit of hope and possibility that so many of us wanted to feel." Looking back on how the speech resonated with both the march and the times, Clarence Jones says: "We caught lightning in a bottle that day."

Fifty years on, the speech still enjoys both national and global acclaim. A survey, conducted in 1999 by researchers at the University of Wisconsin-Madison and Texas A&M, of 137 leading scholars of public address named it the greatest speech of the twentieth century.

During the protests at Tiananmen Square in 1989, some protesters held up posters of King saying "I have a dream." On the wall Israel has built around parts of the West Bank, someone has written: "I have a dream. This is not part of that dream." The phrase "I have a dream" has been spotted in such disparate places as on a train in Budapest and on a mural in suburban Sydney. Asked in 2008 whether they thought the speech was "relevant to people of your generation," 68 percent of Americans said yes, including 76 percent of Blacks and 67 percent of whites. Only 4 percent were not familiar with it.

Why has the speech enjoyed such widespread and lasting resonance? "It was a good speech," says Jones. "Substantively it was not his greatest speech. But it was the power of delivery and the power of the circumstances. The crowd, the march, the Lincoln Memorial, the beautiful day. So many intangible things came together. . . . It was a perfect storm."

✦

A GREAT SPEECH is both timely and timeless. First and foremost it must touch and move its immediate audience. It needs to encapsulate the mood of a moment, reflect, and then amplify it. But it must also simultaneously reach over the heads of the assembled toward posterity. There are many excellent speeches so narrowly tailored to the needs of their particular purpose that their lasting relevance is limited.

The "I Have a Dream" speech qualified on both counts. It was delivered in a year that started with Alabama governor George Wallace standing on the steps of the state capitol in hickory-striped pants and a cutaway coat declaring, "Segregation now, segregation tomorrow, segregation forever," and ended with President Kennedy's assassination. The march was held just ten weeks after Wallace stood in a schoolhouse doorway to prevent Black students from going to college, and little more than two weeks before four Black girls were bombed to death in Birmingham, Alabama, during Sunday school. So it came at a turning point for both the civil rights movement and the country.

The speech starts, both literally and metaphorically, in the shadow of Lincoln (King spoke at the Lincoln Memorial), ends with a quote from a Negro spiritual, and in between quotes the song "My Country 'Tis of Thee" while evoking "a dream rooted in the American dream" and drawing references from the Bible and the Constitution. Within a year of its delivery, Kennedy's successor, Lyndon Johnson, had passed the Civil Rights Act and Cassius Clay had become Muhammad Ali. "It would be like if right now in the Arab Spring somebody made a speech that was fifteen minutes long that summarized what this whole period of social change was all about," one of King's most trusted aides, Andrew Young, told me. "The country was in more turmoil that it had been in since before the Second World War. People didn't understand it. And he explained it.

It wasn't a black speech. It wasn't just a Christian speech. It was an all-American speech."

But the themes of equality, freedom, and solidarity on which it is based are nonetheless universal. They resonate in their own right and can translate into any culture, country, or epoch. It works as well today for the Roma of Eastern Europe as it does for the Shi'a of Bahrain. On its fiftieth anniversary it has aged well, and there is little reason to believe that it won't remain one of the most lauded speeches on the planet in fifty years' time. By any measure—timeliness, timelessness, rhetoric, oratory, cadence, pacing, audience response—it was a great speech. But not all great speeches are deemed historically significant. "History" does not objectively sift through speeches, pick out the best on their merits, and then dedicate them faithfully to public memory. It commits itself to the task with great prejudice and fickle appreciation in a manner that tells us as much about historians and their times as the speech itself.

"The facts of history never come to us pure," writes E. H. Carr in his seminal essay "The Historian and His Facts," "since they do not and cannot exist in pure form: they are always refracted through the mind of the recorder. . . . History means interpretation. . . . It is the historian who has decided for his own reasons that Caesar's crossing of that petty stream, the Rubicon, is a fact of history, whereas the crossing of the Rubicon by millions of other people before or since interests nobody at all."

The speeches we believe to be most decisive can come only from those speeches we have heard about. Those given by a poor woman in Swahili, Kurdish, or Quechua are far less likely to make it through the filter of race, sex, class, and language than those given by wealthy white men in English, French, or Spanish. One wonders whether Nelson Mandela's most famous oration, before his conviction by apartheid South Africa's Supreme Court on April 20, 1964 ("[Nonracial democracy] is an ideal which I hope to live for and to achieve. But if needs be, it is an ideal for which I am prepared to die"), would have been as fondly or well remembered had it been delivered in his native tongue of Xhosa or the nation's most popular first language, Zulu, instead of English, its fourth most widely spoken.

Many fine speeches have been given that we have never heard because they were spoken by people whose words were not deemed worthy of being considered "historical." In October 2002 a relatively junior Illinois state senator called Barack Obama gave a speech against the Iraq War in Chicago that would prove politically important to his presidential pretensions. But there is no television footage of this, because nobody imagined they were listening to a future president. "I would kill for that [footage]," said David Axelrod, Obama's campaign manager. "No one realized at the time that it would be a historic thing."

Technology also plays a role. The relatively recent ability to broadcast on television, radio, and the Internet transforms any speech from something most people would have to either witness firsthand or read later to one almost anyone might see and hear at any time. To be fully appreciated, King's speech must be heard and, to a lesser extent seen. Technology cannot make a bad speech great, but it can make a great speech heard.

✦

MARTIN LUTHER KING delivered many speeches (at least 350 in 1963 alone). Many speeches have been delivered on civil rights and, indeed, were delivered at the March on Washington. So what was it that made this particular speech historical? And what makes it great? Why do we remember it? How do we remember it? What is it about it that we like to remember? And what about it have we chosen to forget?

When King was assassinated in Memphis in 1968 he was not particularly popular and the speech had not gained the legendary status it has today. Both he and the address could have gone the way of many great leaders and addresses and, in the words of Uruguayan writer Eduardo Galeano, been "amputated" from the body of history.

Paradoxically, while the "dream" segment is the most memorable element—so much so that it is most commonly referred to as "the I have a dream speech"—it was never included in King's prepared text. Its addition was extemporaneous. Would the speech have been remembered in the same way, or even at all, if King had not taken that spontaneous turn?

It was not the only compelling refrain in the address. Near the beginning he talks about the United States' reneging on its promises to African Americans: "In a sense we have come to our nation's capital to cash a check . . . a promissory note . . . for life, liberty and the pursuit of happiness" written by the drafters of the Constitution and the Declaration of Independence. He goes on to argue that the country has paid with a bad check and effectively defaulted on its promise. "We refuse to believe that there are insufficient funds in the great vaults of opportunity of this nation," he says. "So we have come to cash this check—a check that will give us upon demand the riches of freedom and the security of justice."

Then, right at the end, he shifts to a riff borrowed from the nineteenth-century patriotic song "My Country 'Tis of Thee," in particular the last line of its first verse: "Let freedom ring." Starting with the more liberal North, he takes the crowd on an evocative tour of the United States, calling for freedom to ring from "the prodigious hilltops of New Hampshire . . . to the curvaceous slopes of California." Finally, he takes a dark turn toward the South, including "every hill and molehill in Mississippi," a state he has earlier described as "sweltering with the heat of injustice."

While neither passage is quite as long as the "I have a dream" section, both are substantial and evocative. "Even the way it's always referred to tells you everything you need to know about what people want to remember," Jack O'Dell, one of King's former aides, told me. "Nobody ever calls it the 'bad check' speech."

Moreover, most who knew King and his work believe he gave at least one speech that deserved as much or perhaps more historical attention than that delivered to the March on Washington. "I think his speech four years later at the Riverside Church in New York, in which he condemned the war in Vietnam and talked about the United States as the greatest purveyor of violence in the world, was by far the best speech of his life in terms of sheer tone and substance," argues Lewis, who is now a congressman.

But to bemoan the absence of King's other great speeches, or other sections of the Washington speech, from public consciousness would be to mistake collective memory as being something other than selective and contingent. To honor King as an antiwar crusader, America would have had to come to terms with its militaristic impulses. Even as it winds down its wars in Iraq and Afghanistan, there seems to have been little resolution on this point. Similarly, to recall King's Washington speech through the metaphor of "the bad check" would demand an engagement with both the material legacy of racism and the material remedy of antiracism—a challenge the country has hardly begun to address.

Venerating his speech at the March on Washington through the dream sequence, however, upholds a positive (albeit metaphorical) diagnosis for an apparently chronic ailment—American racism. As such, it is a rare thing in almost any culture or nation—an optimistic oration about race that acknowledges the desperate circumstances that made it necessary while still projecting hope, patriotism, humanism, and militancy. "The speech explained black people's concerns and demands simply and in an easily understandable fashion that was difficult to rebut," veteran civil rights activist Julian Bond told me. "And among King's many speeches it is easily digestible by a white audience and more palatable to them, as opposed to his antiwar speeches and critiques of capitalism."

In the age of Obama and the Tea Party, there is something in there for everyone. It speaks, in the vernacular of the Black church, with clarity and conviction to African Americans' historical plight and looks forward to a time when that plight would be eliminated. Its nod to all that is sacred in American political culture, from the founding fathers to the American dream, makes it patriotic. It sets bigotry against color-blindness while prescribing no map for how we get from one to the other, simply telling the crowd to go home "knowing that somehow this situation can and will be changed."

These strengths in the breadth of its appeal are also its flaws in terms of depth. It is in no small part appreciated so widely because the interpretations of what King was saying vary so widely. Polls show that while African Americans and American whites agree about the extent to which "the dream has been realized," they profoundly disagree on the state of contemporary race relations. Hearing the same speech, they understand different things.

Conservatives, meanwhile, have been keen to co-opt both King and the speech. In 2010, on the forty-seventh anniversary of the speech, media personality and Tea Party favorite Glenn Beck held the "Restoring Honor" rally at the Lincoln Memorial, telling a crowd of around ninety thousand that "the man who stood down on those stairs ... gave his life for everyone's right to have a dream." Almost a year later Black Republican presidential candidate Herman Cain opened his speech to the Southern Republican Leadership Conference with the words "I have a dream."

Their embrace of the speech, particularly when using elements out of context to challenge affirmative action and civil rights legislation, has made some Black intellectuals and activists wary. "The speech is profoundly and willfully misunderstood," King's longtime friend Vincent Harding told me. "People take the parts that require the least inquiry, the least change, the least work." Many fear that the speech can too easily be distorted in a manner that undermines the speaker's legacy. "In the light of the determined misuse of King's rhetoric, a modest proposal appears in order," Georgetown University professor Michael Eric Dyson has written. "A ten-year moratorium on listening to or reading 'I Have a Dream.' At first blush, such a proposal seems absurd and counterproductive. After all, King's words have convinced many Americans that racial justice should be aggressively pursued. The sad truth is, however, that our political climate has eroded the real point of King's beautiful words."

These responses tell us at least as much about now as then, and perhaps more. The fiftieth anniversary of "I Have a Dream" arrives at a time when the president is Black, whites are destined to become a minority in little more than a generation, and civil rights–era protections are being systematically dismantled. Segregationists have all but disappeared, even if segregation as a lived experience has not. A civil rights movement that could cohere an event like the March on Washington no longer exists. Racism, however, remains, and so long as it does, the debate about its root causes will remain vexed.

In the speech King claims: "Nineteen sixty-three is not an end, but a beginning." In terms of mass, popular, nonracial activism against Jim Crow, it would turn out to be the beginning of the end—a pivotal, seminal milestone in the push for social justice. Fifty years on, it is clear that in eliminating legal segregation—not racism but formal, codified discrimination—the civil rights movement delivered the last moral victory in America for which there is still a consensus. While the struggle to defeat segregation was bitter and divisive, nobody today is seriously campaigning for its return or openly mourning its demise. The speech's appeal lies in the fact that, whatever the interpretation, it remains the most eloquent, poetic, unapologetic, and public articulation of that victory.

1

The Moment

ON FEBRUARY 1, 1960, seventeen-year-old Franklin McCain and three Black friends went to the whites-only counter at Woolworths in Greensboro, North Carolina, and took a seat. "We wanted to go beyond what our parents had done. . . .The worst thing that could happen was that the Ku Klux Klan could kill us . . . but I had no concern for my personal safety. The day I sat at that counter I had the most tremendous feeling of elation and celebration," he told me. "I felt that in this life nothing else mattered. . . . If there's a heaven I got there for a few minutes. I just felt you can't touch me. You can't hurt me. There's no other experience like it."

A few years later, in May 1963, in Birmingham, Alabama, a burly white police officer attempted to intimidate some Black school-children to keep them from joining the growing antisegregation protests. They assured him they knew what they were doing, ignored his entreaties, and continued their march toward Kelly Ingram Park, where they were arrested. A reporter asked one of them her age. "Six," she said, as she climbed into the paddy wagon.

The following month in Mississippi, stalwart civil rights campaigner Fannie Lou Hamer overheard Annell Ponder, a fellow campaigner, being beaten in jail in an adjacent cell.

"Can you say yes, sir, nigger? Can you say yes, sir?" the policeman demanded.

"Yes, I can say yes, sir," replied the protester.

"So say it."

"I don't know you well enough," said Ponder, and then Hamer heard her hit the floor again. The torture continued like this for some time, with Ponder praying for God to forgive her tormentors.

Hamer later recalled that when she next saw Ponder, "one of her eyes looked like blood and her mouth was swollen."

"All books about all revolutions begin with a chapter that describes the decay of tottering authority or the misery and sufferings of the people," wrote the late Polish journalist Ryszard Kapuscinski in *Shah of Shahs*. "They should begin with a psychological chapter, one that shows how a harassed, terrified man suddenly breaks his terror, stops being afraid. This unusual process demands illuminating. Man gets rid of fear and feels free."

The period preceding Martin Luther King's speech at the March on Washington was one such chapter. Until that point there had, of course, been many fearless acts by antiracist protesters. But in that moment the number who were prepared to commit them reached a critical mass. "In three difficult years," wrote the late academic Manning Marable in *Race, Reform and Rebellion*, "the southern struggle had grown from a modest group of black students demonstrating peacefully at one lunch-counter to the largest mass movement for racial reform and civil rights in the twentieth century."

In May 1963, the *New York Times* published more stories about civil rights in two weeks than it had in the previous two years, points out Drew Hansen in *The Dream: Martin Luther King Jr. and the Speech That Inspired a Nation*. According to the Justice Department, during the ten-week period following Kennedy's national address on civil rights in June, shortly before King's speech, there were 758 demonstrations in 186 cities, resulting in 14,733 arrests. Such were the conditions that made the March on Washington possible and King's speech so resonant. As Clarence Jones would later write in *Behind the Dream: The Making of the Speech That Transformed a Nation*: "Text without context, in this case especially, would be quite a loss."

The context was global. Two days after McCain made his protest in Greensboro, the British prime minister Harold Macmillan addressed the South African Parliament in Cape Town with an ominous warning. "The wind of change is blowing through this continent," he said. "Whether we like it or not, this growth of national consciousness is a political fact."

Some, including his immediate audience, did not like it at all. But as the decade wore on, that wind became a gale. In the three years between Macmillan's speech and the March on Washington, Togo, Mali, Senegal, Zaire, Somalia, Benin, Niger, Burkina Faso, Côte d'Ivoire, Chad, Central African Republic, Congo, Gabon, Nigeria, Mauritania, Sierra Leone, Tanganyika, and Jamaica all became independent. Internationally, nonracial democracy and the Black enfranchisement that came with it were the order of the day. The longer

America practiced legal segregation, the more it looked like a slum on the wrong side of history rather than a shining city on the hill. "The new sense of dignity on the part of the Negro," argued King, was due in part to "the awareness that his struggle is a part of a world-wide struggle. He has watched developments in Asia and Africa with rapt attention. . . . [It] is a drama being played out on the stage of the world with spectators and supporters from every continent."

Those places that clung to rigidly codified racism would be increasingly reduced to a rump: South Africa, Namibia, Rhodesia, and Mozambique in Africa; the Deep South in the United States—that region W. J. Cash described, in *The Mind of the South*, as "not quite a nation within a nation, but the next thing to it." From here on, white privilege could be explicitly defended only by resorting to ever more heinous acts of violence that prompted, in response, ever more determined acts of defiance.

"The year before [the March on Washington] had been like a second Civil War," wrote John Lewis in his autobiography, *Walking with the Wind*, "with bombings, beatings and killings happening almost weekly. A march would be met with violence, which would cause yet another march, and so on. That was the pattern."

As the segregationists' violence escalated, so did the militancy of Black activists. Earlier that year King had been heckled in Harlem with the chant "We want Malcolm, we want Malcolm."

As long as there has been racism in America, there has been a rift between those who sought to fight alongside whites for equality and integration on the one hand and on the other Black nationalists, who argued that Blacks should organize separately from whites to establish an autonomous homeland either within the United States or in Africa. For some the issue was tactical, for others a matter of principle, providing for plenty of overlap between the two. At this time Malcolm X was the most prominent Black nationalist and a member of the Nation of Islam, a Muslim sect that did not believe in nonviolence or integration.

"It's just like when you've got some coffee that's too black, which means it's too strong," Malcolm X once said, explaining his wariness about working with white people. "What do you do? You integrate it with cream, you make it weak. But if you pour too much cream in it, you won't even know you ever had coffee. It used to be hot, it becomes cool. It used to be strong, it becomes weak. It used to wake you up, now it puts you to sleep."

By the summer of 1963 some African Americans were losing hope that white America would ever accommodate their most basic demands for human rights. "There were many in the summer of '63 who did [agree with Malcolm X]—more it seemed every day," wrote Lewis. "I could see Malcolm's appeal, especially to young people who had never been exposed to or had any understanding of the discipline of non-violence—and also to people who had given up on that discipline. There was no question Malcolm X was tapping into a growing feeling of restlessness and resentment among America's blacks."

On May 13, John F. Kennedy's principal Black adviser, Louis Martin, wrote a memo to the president, explaining: "As this is written, demonstrations and marches are planned. The accelerated tempo of Negro restiveness . . . may soon create the most critical state of race relations this country has seen since the Civil War." A month later the US ambassador to India, J. K. Galbraith, urged: "This is our last chance to remain in control of matters."

While such warnings were portentous, this was no existential threat. The American state was not about to be overthrown. Nonetheless, the moment represented a thoroughgoing assault against one of the fundamental pillars on which the nation had been established: white supremacy.

One of the central aims of the civil rights movement was to create a crisis in the polity. This strategy was explicitly laid out by James Farmer, the head of the Congress of Racial Equality (CORE) in 1961 during the Freedom Rides, when a racially mixed group of protesters went through the South on buses with Blacks sitting at the front and whites at the back. "What we had to do," said Farmer, "was make it more dangerous politically for the federal government not to enforce the law than it would be for them to enforce federal law. We felt we could count on the racists of the South to create a crisis so that the federal government would be compelled to enforce the law."

The white citizenry of the South was only too happy to oblige. When one bus rolled into Anniston, Alabama, it was chased up the highway and firebombed. When another arrived in Birmingham, it was met by men wielding baseball bats and lead pipes. These attacks took place with the active collusion of the region's political class. Alabama's governor, George Wallace, took office in the year of King's speech. Shortly before he did so, his attorney general, Richmond Flowers, warned him of the predictable consequences of following through on the defiant segregationist rhetoric that had been a hallmark of his election campaign. "Look George, you gonna be whupped all through the courts. And when you're whupped in the courts, the Klan's gonna come out on the streets and the killing's gonna start. You know that's what's gonna happen."

Wallace told him, "Damnit, send the Justice Department word, I ain't compromising with anybody. I'm gonna make 'em bring troops into this state."

A populist and a demagogue, Wallace aimed not to score a substantial victory but to perform resistance; a strategy that, a century after the Confederate defeat in the Civil War, had particular appeal among a section of southern whites. "Wallace's political psychology essentially derives from the Southern romance of an unvanquished and intransigent spirit in the face of utter, desolate defeat," argues Marshall Frady in *Wallace*.

What Farmer could not have predicted, however, was just how reluctant the federal government under Kennedy would be to intervene when faced with these crises. This was partly because the members of his administration didn't fully comprehend the enormity of what was happening. JFK's brother, US attorney general Robert Kennedy, evidently struggled to grasp the indignity of segregation. "They can stand at the lunch counters. They don't have to eat there. They can pee before they come into the store or the supermarket." Nor was he particularly sympathetic to Black people's impatience with the slow pace of change. "Negroes are now just antagonistic and mad and they're going to be mad at everything. You can't talk to them. . . . My friends all say [even] the Negro maids and servants are getting antagonistic."

The president, meanwhile, was worried about alienating a key sector of his electoral base: white southerners. The Democratic Party at that time was a curious coalition of southern segregationists, northern liberals, and those African Americans who were allowed to vote. The Black vote had been crucial to Kennedy's narrow victory against Nixon in 1960, but so too were southern whites. Both Wallace and King had voted for Kennedy.

From the outset, the president decided the wisest strategy was to avoid coming between them. "Kennedy now worried that any attempt to push Southern Democrats on civil rights was likely to produce a backlash," writes Nick Bryant in *The Bystander: John F. Kennedy and the Struggle for Black Equality*. "If we drive . . . moderate southerners to the wall with a lot of civil rights demands that can't pass anyway," Kennedy told an aide, "then what happens to the Negro on minimum wages, housing and the rest?"

But in the absence of federal intervention the crisis didn't disappear; it deepened. African Americans became more determined; segregationists became more desperate. "The crisis," argued Italian Marxist Antonio Gramsci in his *Prison Notebooks*, "consists precisely in the fact that the old is dying and the new cannot be born."

Until the summer of 1963, when King delivered his speech, even though the health of the old segregated polity in the South was clearly failing, the birth of a new integrated one had yet to be induced. Eventually the Kennedy administration was forced to play midwife. It had no choice. By the time of the March on Washington the civil rights movement had raised acute questions of power: Who has it? Who wants it? How do you get it? How do you keep it? The answers would be delivered in the bluntest fashion. Governors personally blocked schoolhouse doors, cities were put under martial law, National Guard troops were federalized and dispatched, children filled jails, protesters were killed. In short, the fundamental ability and right of the state to maintain law and order became an open question, assaulted at every turn from all directions.

In the South, segregation had been the norm for more than two centuries, with a brief break during Reconstruction after the Civil War. While it had always been resisted, generations of both Blacks and whites, not to mention officials both federal and local, had grown accustomed to it. "Who hears a clock tick or the surf murmur or the trains pass?" asked James Kilpatrick, editor of the *New Leader*, of Richmond, Virginia, in *The Southern Case for School Segregation* in 1962. "Not those who live by the clock or the sea or the track. In the South, the acceptance of racial separation begins in the cradle. What rational man imagines this concept can be shattered overnight?"

Now, with the status quo openly challenged and brutally defended, long-held allegiances were tested and positions polarized. Key players who had learned to live with segregation—the federal government, business interests, liberal whites, conservative Blacks— were forced to reckon with the arrival of a new order. And fissures opened up not just between these various interested parties but also within them as events tested their ability to accommodate, negotiate, and confront this impending transformation, drawing sharp distinctions at each juncture between those who ostensibly held power and those who actually wielded influence.

✦

IN FEW PLACES were these developments clearer or more pivotal to both the March on Washington and King's speech than Birmingham, Alabama, during the spring of 1963. Birmingham, nicknamed Bombingham because of the violent attacks on Black leaders' homes, was one of the most violent and racist cities in the South. In *Eyes on the Prize*, Juan Williams tells how in 1956 Nat King Cole had been beaten there while performing on stage; a year later a car full of drunk whites castrated a man they'd snatched from a street corner. "Nothing at that time would have surprised me about Alabama," the late Fred Shuttlesworth, the leading civil rights figure in the town, told me. "It was just Mississippi moved a little to the east. White people there used to do things first and then think about it later. Even the most liberal white people there supported segregation."

Shuttlesworth invited King to Birmingham because he knew that where King went the cameras were sure to follow. King came, in no small part, because the previous year he had suffered a crushing defeat in Albany, Georgia, where he had been outmaneuvered by local authorities, and he thought Birmingham could help revive his reputation.

Despite the city's notoriety, indeed partly because of it, there was some reason to believe they could mount a successful challenge to segregation there. Birmingham's white community was split, primarily between business and political interests. Both supported segregation, but their relationship to it was different. Politicians were dependent on segregation for their authority, which they maintained through force or the threat of it. The business community was primarily interested in profits. Integration would result in a sharp increase in Black voters, who would threaten the stranglehold of white politicians. But it would also give rights to Black consumers and open up the labor market, which could, under the right circumstances, help commerce. The violence meted out by the politicians, meanwhile, could now be broadcast both nationally and internationally, sullying the city's image in a way that was bad for business. When asked at a press conference why he thought Birmingham would prove more successful than Albany, King retorted: "The Negro has enough buying power in Birmingham to make the difference between profit and loss in any business. That was not true in Albany, Georgia." So there was less at stake for the business community in accommodating integration than there was for politicians.

"In a highly industrialized, 20th-century civilization, we hit Jim Crow precisely where it was most anachronistic, dispensable, and vulnerable—in hotels, lunch counters, terminals, libraries, swimming pools, and the like," wrote Bayard Rustin two years later. "For in these forms, Jim Crow does impede the flow of commerce in the broadest sense: it is a nuisance in a society on the move (and on the make)."

In 1962, for example, a student boycott forced some local stores to take down segregationist signs and integrate lunch counters, toilets, and water fountains. Eugene "Bull" Connor, Birmingham's safety commissioner and head of the segregationist triumvirate running the city, had responded by citing the stores in question for building-code violations. The signs soon went back up.

That year Sid Smyer, the president of the local chamber of commerce, along with other businessmen, launched an effort to change the city's government structure from a cabal of three segregationist commissioners to an elected mayor and nine city councilmen. "You might say it was a dollar and cents thing," Smyer told Howell Raines in *My Soul Is Rested*. "If we're going to have good business in Birmingham, we better change our way of living." Voters approved his proposal and in 1963 elected Albert Boutwell over

Connor. Connor then petitioned the courts, demanding that he be allowed to complete his term.

This inevitably resulted in confusion. There was not so much a power vacuum as a power glut. "On Tuesdays the [old] Commission met . . . and proceeded to govern the city, and when they finished, they would march out and [the] nine [new] council members would march in, and they would proceed to adopt laws and spend money and conduct the affairs of the city," former Birmingham mayor David Vann told Juan Williams. For a while both Boutwell and Connor signed city employees' checks.

But if the city's white power structure was fractured between those who favored confrontation and those who sought some form of accommodation, Black leadership in the city was no less so. Some local Black businessmen and more conservative clergy were not happy about King's arrival or the escalation of activism, believing the new administration should be given the chance to show its commitment to reform.

On April 3 the *Birmingham News* announced Boutwell's victory over Connor with a front-page picture showing a bright sun rising over the city and the caption "New Day Dawns for Birmingham." That morning King launched Project C—for confrontation. Shortly after 10 a.m., writes Bryant, around sixty-five protesters sat in at lunch counters across the city. Four establishments simply turned off the lights and announced they were closed; one called the police. The protests continued for several days, landing 150 demonstrators in prison but making little impact. A circuit court judge issued an injunction forbidding King, Ralph Abernathy, and 131 other civil rights leaders from taking part in further demonstrations. They had run out of money to bail out the jailed and out of ideas for attracting publicity. King was at a loss. Sitting with his advisers in the Black-owned Gaston Motel, he said: "Look, I don't know what to do. I just know that something has got to change in Birmingham. I don't know whether I can raise money to get people out of jail. I do know that I can go into jail with them." He then headed out to lead a demonstration and was promptly arrested and put in solitary confinement.

It was there he wrote his now famous *Letter from Birmingham Jail*, a response to eight white Birmingham clergymen who had criticized the demonstrations as ill-timed and inflammatory. "Frankly I have yet to engage in a direct-action campaign that was 'well-timed' in the view of those who have not suffered unduly from the disease of segregation," King responded caustically, writing on toilet paper and in the margins of a newspaper. This argument captured one of the key tensions of the political moment: many whites, ostensibly sympathetic to equality, wanted the civil rights activists to slow down, while the activists insisted things were going too slowly. It was an argument King would pick up again at the March on Washington. "We have also come to this hallowed spot to remind America of the fierce urgency of now," he said in his most famous speech. "This is no time to engage in the luxury of cooling off or to take the tranquilizing drug of gradualism."

King was held in jail for nine days. The campaign was waning. Birmingham's white leaders, the Kennedy administration, and important figures in the local Black community wanted him to leave town. Instead he decided to double down on his presence there by escalating Project C. This time the shock troops were to be the one group that did not rely on white people for work and had no dependents to support or jobs to lose—kids. King's aides asked Black schoolchildren around the city to watch a film about a student sit-in, called *The Nashville Story*, at their local churches and then decide if they wanted to join in nonviolent protests.

They were pushing at an open door. "When we left school to participate in the demonstrations, it was one of those things, you know, if your cousin, your brother, your sister, your best friend left school, you left school with them," Dennis Mallory, who was a teenager in Birmingham at the time, told me. "Me and my friend says OK, we're leaving, and when that day came we got up and we left and we came, knowing the purpose was to go to jail. It did not scare me because I was with people that I was with every day. I think my school had about three hundred participants in the children's march, and as it turned out I got arrested and was in a jail cell— there were twelve people in the jail cell . . . eleven were from my school. So it was like being at school every day. I think the fear factor was kind of gone because you're in this jail cell, of course, but you're in there with people you saw and talked to every day."

According to Rustin, this attitude exemplified both King's appeal and explained his ability to mobilize large numbers quickly. The Southern Christian Leadership Conference (SCLSC), which King headed, was less a mass organization than a loosely tied group of affiliates that generally did his bidding.

"All King needed around him were people who had hard asses and perseverance," Rustin once said. "They didn't have to have a pea in their head as long as they would sit down and be arrested and sit down on their hard behinds and persevere again. I know Martin very well . . . he did not have the ability to organize vampires to go to a bloodbath. The organization was done by Southern brutality."

They called the first day of children's protests—Thursday May 2—D-Day. City leader Bull Connor was overwhelmed at first but soon ordered mass arrests. By the afternoon 959 people, most of them children, were in jail. Friday they called Double D-Day. This time Connor was ready. The children made their way out of the Sixteenth Street Baptist Church toward Kelly Ingram Park. When they refused to turn back, firemen pounded them with hoses delivering one-hundred-pound jets of water. They then added an attachment that doubled the force, making the hoses powerful enough to rip the bark off a tree from thirty yards. When Black onlookers threw bricks and bottles at the firemen, Connor set dogs on them.

Scenes of children set upon by German shepherd dogs and knocked off their feet by water cannons provided some of the most dramatic television footage of the entire era. Those in town who had counseled moderation now had to pick sides. Arthur Gaston, owner of the motel in which King was staying—and one of Birmingham's more conservative African Americans, who had originally appealed for King to stay away—was on the phone to David Vann, one of the city's more liberal whites, when he switched topics mid-sentence: "But lawyer Vann, they've turned the fire hoses on a little black girl. And they're rolling that girl right down the middle of the street." Gaston hung up.

The impact of the violence was amplified by the recent arrival of near-ubiquitous television coverage. In 1954, when the Supreme Court banned segregation, just 56 percent of American homes had televisions; by 1963 it was 91 percent. And events in Birmingham made for riveting viewing. "It was a masterpiece [in] the use of media to explain a cause to the general public," Vann told Williams in *Eyes on the Prize*. "In those days, we had 15 minutes of national news and 15 minutes of local news, and in marching only one block they could get enough news film to fill all of the newscasts of all the television stations in the United States."

The television audience had also expanded internationally, a fact that three months later would enable the March on Washington to gain global attention. "A technological breakthrough greatly expanded the day's audience well beyond the nation's shores," write Gene Roberts and Hank Klibanoff in *The Race Beat: The Press, the Civil Rights Struggle and the Awakening of a Nation*. "Telstar, a communications satellite launched in July 1962, took live coverage of the march to six countries; Communist nations received the coverage and taped it but did not show it live. Television networks in West Germany, Japan and France sent their own crews to Washington."

Telegenic as he was, Kennedy's ability to project the youth, glamour, and vitality of the "free world" was overshadowed by the brutal scenes coming out of Birmingham, especially at a time when the Cold War had already put America's international reputation under close scrutiny.

There was barely a moment during his brief presidency when he was not confronted with crisis. Within seven months of his taking office, construction began on the Berlin Wall, and an attempt at fomenting a coup in Cuba, where the revolution had succeeded just two years before, had failed miserably. The Cuban Missile Crisis, less than a year before the March on Washington, had brought the Cold War to his doorstep and the world to the brink of nuclear catastrophe. On the day of the march, he met with advisers to discuss whether to back a coup in Vietnam.

And as Kennedy lectured the world on democratic values, here was evidence in Birmingham that the United States was seeking to export something it could not grow at home. His administration knew it. "This nation is confronted with one of the gravest issues we have faced since 1865, and that issue of race relations deeply affects the conduct of our foreign policy relations," said Secretary of State Dean Rusk. "I am speaking of the problem of discrimination. . . . Our voice is muted, our friends are embarrassed, our enemies are gleeful. . . . We are running this race with one of our legs in a cast."

King knew it too. "The United States is concerned about its image," he said. "When things started happening down here, Mr. Kennedy got disturbed. For Mr. Kennedy . . . is battling for the minds of men in Asia and Africa—some one billion in the neutralist sector of the world—and they aren't gonna respect the United States of America if she deprives men and women of the basic rights of life because of the color of their skin. Mr. Kennedy knows that."

On May 9 the official newspaper of the Soviet Communist Party, *Pravda*, ran a piece about Birmingham headlined "Monstrous Crimes among Racists in the United States." Later in the year Chinese leader Mao Zedong branded the Kennedy administration "the chief culprit for the ruthless persecution of Negroes, champion of racial discrimination, and main source of policy of oppression and aggression throughout the world."

Aware that the situation was spiraling out of control, Kennedy had no choice but to intervene, albeit gingerly at first. He sent Burke

Marshall, the US assistant attorney general, to Alabama to negotiate a settlement. Shuttlesworth, who had been injured after being knocked down by one of the hoses, was in the hospital. Marshall negotiated with King and the local white merchants. For the business community it was primarily a pragmatic decision. They clinched a deal that would bring about the desegregation of lunch counters and the end to demonstrations in the city and planned a press conference to announce it.

But this agreement wasn't without its difficulties. In particular it raised questions about the ability of those who negotiated it to maintain credibility with the people they claimed to be negotiating for. This was a challenge no less great for the civil rights leaders than it was for the segregationists and business leaders. Though they had made a deal, it was by no means clear that the "leaders" on either side were in any position to deliver. Each had to contend with impatience and militancy from below that risked spinning out of their control.

When Shuttlesworth, still recuperating on his sickbed, heard of the truce, he was livid. As far as he was concerned King had settled for too little too soon. "If you and Kennedy [announce that deal], then I will get out of my sickbed and start the demonstrations right up again. They might be calling you Mr. King now, but they will be calling you Mr. Shit when I've finished." When Marshall attempted to convince Shuttlesworth, telling him that promises had already been made, Shuttlesworth turned his wrath on him. "Who gave you the authority to make any promises to any people without clearing it?" he asked. "But if you made promises you can go back now and tell 'em that the demonstrations'll be on, 'cause you cain't call 'em off. President Kennedy cain't call 'em off, and there's Martin

Luther King—he cain't call 'em off."

King talked him around. A press conference was held, promoting the plan. Now Connor was livid. Denouncing the agreement as a "capitulation by certain weak-kneed white people under the threat of violence by the rabble-rousing Negro, King," he called on whites to boycott the stores in question.

The next evening, May 11, the Klan held a meeting outside town. "Martin Luther King's epitaph . . . can be written here in Birmingham," said the Grand Dragon, the highest-ranking Klansman in the state. Not long afterward bombs ripped through the Gaston Motel, where King had been staying (but he had left that day), as well as at King's brother's house in town. Hearing the commotion, Black people poured out of their homes, dance halls, and bars and gathered at both sites. Rioting soon spread over a twenty-eight-block area as some in the crowd threw rocks at the police. Six stores and a two-story apartment building were burned down, and several cars were overturned and set ablaze. One policeman chased a protester down an alleyway and emerged with three knife wounds in his back. That moment Ryszard Kapuscinski describes when "a terrified man stops . . . being afraid" had arrived, upending the established order.

One local minister, Abraham Wood, recalls an incident behind the Gaston Motel, where a Black man shook a long knife at a policeman and said, "I want that suit you got on. Gimme that suit." "I've seen the time when the policeman would have dashed there and got that Negro," Wood told Raines. "Policeman didn't move, just looked at him, and he didn't go. The black man tried to get him. 'You come on back here,' [the man said in a soft beckoning voice]. Policeman didn't go."

State troopers arrived, effectively putting the city under martial law imposed by Wallace and Connor. "Let the whole fucking city burn," yelled one rioter. "This'll show those white mother-fuckers."

This risked escalating the entire conflict to another level. The one thing that had prevented a descent into a vicious cycle of recrimination and retribution had been the civil rights leadership's insistence on nonviolence. This was not merely a strategic ploy on the part of King, his entourage, and beyond in the movement. It was a deeply held principle. But while it was widely advocated among the leadership, the attachment to nonviolence among the base was less secure. "Nonviolence is hard," Joan Baez, the renowned folk singer who performed at the March on Washington, told me. "You don't know for sure that it won't get you killed. All you know is that you won't kill someone else."

The philosophy had been sorely tested by the white segregationists and slammed by more militant Black voices. "I am for violence," said Malcolm X, "if nonviolence means we continue postponing a solution to the American black man's problem just to avoid violence." The scenes from Birmingham, which Malcolm X referred to repeatedly, gave this message more resonance. "If a dog is biting a black man," he said, "the black man should kill the dog, whether the dog is a police dog or a hound dog or any kind of dog. If a dog is fixed on a black man when that black man is doing nothing but trying to take advantage of what the government says is supposed to be his, then that black man should kill that dog or any two-legged dog who sets the dog on him."

Neither Malcolm X nor the Nation of Islam had been associated with violence beyond rhetoric and internal feuds. But as Lewis has pointed out (see p. 19 above), that didn't stop their defiant tone from gaining traction. Rosa Parks, an ostensibly demure icon of the movement, met Malcolm X shortly before his assassination in February 1965 and stated afterward that her philosophy was closer to his than to King's. "Dr. King used to say that black people should receive brutality with love, and I believed that was a goal to work for, but I couldn't reach that point in my mind at all."

The reaction of Maya Angelou and her fellow African American émigrés in Ghana to the news that King would lead a march on Washington was scathing precisely because they felt nonviolence had not worked: "All the prayers, sit-ins, sacrifices, jail sentences, humiliation, insults and jibes had not borne out Reverend King's vision," wrote Angelou in *All God's Children Need Traveling Shoes*. "When maddened White citizens and elected political leaders vowed to die before they would see segregation come to an end, I became more resolute in rejecting nonviolence and more adamant in denying Martin Luther King." This attitude was all the more damning because Angelou had actually worked for the SCLC just a few years before.

That viewpoint was shared by one of the guests of honor at the March on Washington, the nation's first Black flight attendant, Carol Taylor, who said of King: "The white male media presents him as the peaceful black man, turning the other cheek. Me, being a roustabout, I am not too sanguine about the efficacy of someone turning the other cheek. Here you have the police force almost daily slaughtering black males. Malcolm said, 'When you pull a knife halfway out, don't tell me to thank you.'"

King makes reference to this in his speech at the march: "There is something that I must say to my people who stand on the warm threshold which leads into the palace of justice," he says. "In the process of gaining our rightful place we must not be guilty of wrongful deeds. . . . Again and again we must rise to the majestic heights of meeting physical force with soul force."

This was not a passage simply to placate his critics. It was included because violent retaliation by African Americans posed a genuine threat to King's authority. In Birmingham he was barely able to pull things back from the brink. He returned to town, trawling the pool halls and bars to collect knives and calm tempers. Kennedy dispatched three thousand troops to be on standby seventy-five miles away at Fort McClellan. The truce held, and with the agreement honored, King left.

✦

"THE REVOLUTIONARIES," Hannah Arendt once argued in an interview, "are those who know when power is lying in the street and when they can pick it up." The civil rights leaders were quick to recognize the potential to seize the initiative following Birmingham. "The events in Birmingham were more important for organizing [the March on Washington] than . . . me or anything else," said Rustin at the time. "The civil rights movement has reached yet a new stage in its development. For the first time a thoroughgoing revolution is occurring in the South. . . . The Negro community is now fighting for total freedom. . . . The Negro masses are no longer prepared to wait for anybody. . . . They are going to move. Nothing can stop them."

The public was now fully sensitized to the urgency and gravity of the nation's racial problems in a way it had not been before. Previously, only 4 percent of Americans regarded civil rights as the country's most pressing issue; after Birmingham it was 52 percent. "Never before," writes historian Taylor Branch, "was a country transformed, arguably redeemed, by the active moral witness of schoolchildren."

While embracing nonviolence had been required for the civil rights movement to get a hearing from Kennedy and, to some degree, earn his trust, it was the battles on Birmingham's streets that finally forced him to act. "It was the black on white violence of May 11 . . . that represented the real watershed moment in Kennedy's thinking and the turning point in administration policy," writes Nick Bryant. "Kennedy had grown used to segregationist attacks against civil rights protestors. But he . . . was far more troubled by black mobs running amok. Based on his fraught exchanges . . . that afternoon it is clear that it was this fear that prompted him to reconsider his civil rights proposals, and to push soon afterwards for far stronger measures."

The only people who didn't realize by this time that segregation's days were numbered were the segregationists—a powerful but dwindling minority, particularly within the political class. For everyone else the question was what that number might look like— one hundred days or one thousand? Some, particularly within the administration, favored a gradual transition that would cause minimal social disruption. Others, particularly the young Black activists, believed change had to occur straightaway and only massive social disruption could achieve it.

And then there was the question of what would replace segregation, which, as applied to the South, was something of a misnomer.

Black and white people's lives there had been intimately connected. Black women breastfed white babies, slaves sometimes lived in the same houses as masters, and white men routinely slept with Black women. In 1948 the late South Carolina senator Strom Thurmond had stood for the presidency as a segregationist. "On the question of social intermingling of the races, our people draw the line," he said. But the line was neither straight nor true. At the time Thurmond had a twenty-three-year-old Black daughter by a former maid. The question was not whether Black and white people could mix—they were doing that already—but rather the basis on which they mixed.

"The issue for Black people was never integration or segregation, but white supremacy. The paradigm of integration and segregation was a white concern," says Charles Payne, Frank P. Dixon Distinguished Service Professor at the University of Chicago. "That was how they posed the issue of civil rights given their own interests, and that was how the entire issue then became understood. But the central concerns of Black people were not whether they should integrate with white people or not, but how to challenge white people's hold on the power structure." Birmingham had shown that the civil rights movement was capable of mounting an effective challenge—but only when sufficient pressure was applied from below.

The full extent of the precariousness and potential of the moment was revealed in just twenty-four hours starting early on June 11, 1963, a few months before the march. That Tuesday began with Bobby Kennedy examining maps of the University of Alabama's Tuscaloosa campus as his three young children played at his feet. A couple of hours later two Black students, Vivian Malone and James

Hood, tried to register for classes on campus. In a choreographed piece of brinkmanship, Governor Wallace stood at the entrance to Foster Auditorium, flanked by state troopers, to refuse them entry. The students went to their dorms while Deputy Attorney General Nicholas Katzenbach ordered Wallace to allow them in. Wallace refused and delivered a speech on states' rights that did not once mention integration or race. President Kennedy then federalized the National Guard and ordered Wallace's removal. "Sir, it is my sad duty to ask you to step aside under the orders of the president of the United States," said General Henry Graham. Wallace made another quick announcement and stepped aside, and Malone and Hood registered.

The sequence of events, if not the precise rendering of them, had been agreed beforehand. "They knew he would step aside," Cully Clark, author of *The Schoolhouse Door: Segregation's Last Stand at the University of Alabama*, told NPR. "I think the fundamental question was how." Troops had practiced the manner in which they would physically lift the governor out of the doorway, just in case.

"It had been little more than a ceremony of futility," writes Marshall Frady. "And, as a historical moment, a rather pedestrian production. But no other Southern governor had managed to strike even that dramatic a pose of defiance and it has never been required of Southern popular heroes that they be successful. Indeed Southerners tend to love their heroes more for their losses."

The previous day the president's inner circle had been divided on whether he should deliver a televised national address on the issues raised by the governor's impending protest. Given the delicacy of the arrangements that had been made to deal with events in Tuscaloosa, they decided to wait and see how things went. After the incident had passed with more theater than chaos, they unanimously advised that the speech was now unnecessary.

Kennedy decided to ignore them, calling executives at the three television networks himself to request airtime. Bryant describes how, with only six hours to write the speech, Kennedy's team struggled to pull together anything coherent. Minutes before the cameras rolled, all they had was a bundle of typed pages interspersed with illegible scribbles. Kennedy's secretary had no time to type up a final version, and his speechwriters had not come up with a conclusion.

With the cameras on, Kennedy started reading from the text; for the last four minutes, he improvised with lines he'd used before from the campaign trail and elsewhere.

What emerged was a message that framed America's racial problem not primarily as one of economic and political power or the legacy of slavery but, literally, as a lack of common "human decency." As such it was explicitly aimed at white Americans. "If an American, because his skin is dark, cannot eat lunch in a restaurant open to the public, if he cannot send his children to the best public school available, if he cannot vote for the public officials who will represent him, if, in short, he cannot enjoy the full and free life which all of us want, then who among us would be content to have the color of his skin changed and stand in his place? Who among us would then be content with the counsels of patience and delay?"

Kennedy went on to reflect on issues of Black unemployment and the slow pace of integration. He spoke of how the South was embarrassing the nation in front of its Cold War adversaries and made the case for equal opportunity. He asked Congress "to enact legislation giving all Americans the right to be served in facilities which are open to the public—hotels, restaurants, theaters, retail stores, and similar establishments. This seems to me to be an elementary right."

"The speech was the most courageous of Kennedy's presidency," writes Bryant. "After two years of equivocation on the subject of civil rights, Kennedy had finally sought to mobilize that vast body of Americans who had long considered segregation immoral, and who were certainly unprepared to countenance the most extreme forms of discrimination."

But it also further tilted the already fragile balance between southern segregationists and northern liberals in the Democratic Party. "For all practical purposes, manuevering to save the Southern vote ended when Kennedy gave his June 11th speech," writes Charles Euchner in *Nobody Turn Me Around*. The next day southern Democrats would respond by defeating a routine funding bill. "[Civil rights] is overwhelming the whole, the whole program," House Majority Leader Carl Albert told the president. "I couldn't do a damn thing with them."

Myrlie Evers had watched the presidential address in bed with her three children before her husband, Medgar, arrived home just after midnight. Medgar was the field secretary of the state's chapter of the National Association for the Advancement of Colored People (the oldest civil rights organization in the country) and was returning from a meeting with activists in a local church, carrying white T-shirts announcing "Jim Crow Must Go."

Lurking in the honeysuckle bushes across the road with a 30.06 bolt-action Winchester hunting rifle was Byron DeLa Beckwith, a fertilizer salesman and Klan member from nearby Greenwood. The sound of Evers slamming the car door was followed rapidly by a burst of gunfire. Myrlie ran downstairs while the children assumed the position they had learned to adopt if their house ever came under attack. When she got to the front door, Medgar's body was slumped in front of her. A bullet had gone through his back and exited through his chest. Just a few hours later he was pronounced dead.

On the day of Medgar Evers's funeral, around a thousand Black youths marched through town, joined later by their elders. When police ordered them to disperse, scuffles broke out. The crowd chanted: "We want the killer." Meeting their demand should not have been difficult. The rifle that was fired was traced to Beckwith, whose fingerprints were on its telescopic sight. Some witnesses reported seeing a man who fit his description in the area that night, as well as a car that looked like his white Plymouth Valiant. As if that weren't enough, he'd openly bragged to fellow Klansmen about carrying out the shooting. Though it took several weeks, he was eventually arrested on the strength of this overwhelming evidence and was charged with the murder. But then matters took an all too predictable turn. Not once but twice in the course of 1964, all-white juries failed to reach a verdict. Beckwith was arrested again in 1990 and finally found guilty in 1994. He wore a Confederate flag pin throughout the hearings. He died in prison in 2001.

✦

IN MANY WAYS these two events, Wallace's otiose performance and Beckwith's murderous assault, typified the segregationists' endgame: a series of dramatic, often violent acts perpetrated by the local state or its ideological surrogates, with no strategic value beyond symbolizing resistance and inciting a response. They were not intended to stop integration but to protest its inevitability. And while those protests were futile, they nonetheless retained the ability to provoke, as the disturbances following the bombing of the Gaston Motel in Birmingham and Evers's funeral testified. The years to come were sufficiently volatile that even ostensibly minor events such as a traffic stop in Watts, Los Angeles, or the raid of a late-night drinking den in Detroit could spark major unrest. The violence and chaos that ensued polarized communities not on issues of ideology or strategy but on the basis of race, weakening the already dim prospects for solidarity across the color line.

"When Medgar was felled by that shot," recalled Myrlie, who went on to dedicate her life to nonviolent interracial activism, "and I rushed out and saw him lying there and people from the neighborhood began to gather, there were also some whose color happened to be white. I don't think I have ever hated as much in my life as I did at that particular moment anyone who had white skin."

At a rapid clip, the center of gravity of Black politics migrated from the South to the North, from rural to urban, middle age to youth, God to Mao, and from integrated, interracial nonviolent struggle to race-based, Black nationalist militancy that accepted violence as a possible strategy. In 1966 Stokely Carmichael, then of the Student Non-Violent Co-ordinating Committee, a grassroots civil rights organization, made his first appeal for Black Power, explaining:

"It is a call for black people in this country to unite, to recognize their heritage, to build a sense of community. It is a call for black people to begin to define their own goals, to lead their own organizations." The same year saw the birth in Oakland, California, of the Black Panther Party for Self-Defense, which advocated armed resistance against police brutality and was influenced by Maoism.

These divisions, and the strains on the strategy of nonviolence they illustrated, would be compounded by the brutal unraveling of the decade. President Kennedy was shot dead just a few months after the March on Washington; Malcolm X was assassinated in 1965; in 1968 both King and Bobby Kennedy were gunned down. And as the Vietnam War escalated and the draft was expanded, an entire generation would be trained and brutalized in violence. Watts went up in flames in 1965; two years later tanks rolled through Detroit's residential areas to quell riots; King's assassination at a motel in Memphis sparked disturbances throughout the country; and in 1970 the National Guard shot and killed four students, some of whom were protesting President Richard Nixon's Cambodia bombing campaign, on the campus of Kent State University in Ohio. Under these circumstances, the notion that Black America alone should pledge itself to nonviolence seemed unrealistic to many.

✦

IN MALONE AND HOOD'S registration at the University of Alabama on June 11, 1963, we see the doors to higher education, and through them career advancement, reluctantly being opened for the small section of Black America that was in a position at that time to reap the fruits of integration. There had been a middle class in Black America for a long time, but as long as segregation existed the material benefits deriving from that status were significantly circumscribed, particularly in the South. Race overwhelmed almost everything. A Black doctor or dentist could not live outside particular neighborhoods, eat in certain establishments, or be served in certain stores. Whatever class differences existed within the Black community, and there were many, they were inevitably subsumed under the broader struggle for equality.

"People remember how good it used to be," recalled Franklin McCain. "But it was hell. Sure, there were some advantages. There was the dentist who lived next door to the ditch digger who lived next door to the preacher before economic stratification started to happen. But that's not right either. It's not at all good for someone who has been working hard to get where they are in their profession to be forced to live in a shack."

With integration, however, came the fracturing of communities as those equipped to take advantage of the new opportunities forged ahead, leaving the rest to struggle. Wealthier people could move to the suburbs; their kids could integrate in white schools and from there go on to top universities. But this success brought its own challenges.

Alongside the few that made it to college were the many, both North and South, whom segregation had undereducated and ill-equipped to find gainful employment in the late twentieth century. A few years after the march, King told a crowd in Chicago, "Let's face the facts: Most of us are going to be living in the ghetto five, ten years from now. But we've got to get some things straightened out right away. I'm not going to wait a month to get the rats and roaches out of my house. Morally, we ought to have what we say in the slogan: Freedom Now. But it all doesn't come now. That's a sad fact of life you have to live with."

At the time of the march, Black unemployment stood at 11 percent, twice the rate of whites (the same gap as exists today). A Black family earned, on average, $3,500 a year, compared to $6,500 for its white counterpart. After civil rights legislation passed, Black Americans no longer fell afoul of the law of the land, but they still remained on the wrong side of the law of probability. More likely to be arrested, convicted, and imprisoned, less likely to be employed, promoted, and educated, most Black Americans did not find that the end of segregation felt like the liberation that had been promised. After the Watts riots King told Rustin: "You know, Bayard, I worked to get these people the right to eat hamburgers, and now I've got to do something . . . to help them get the money to buy them."

With Kennedy's appeal for legislation we saw the shift in focus moving from the streets of Birmingham to Washington's corridors of power. This was progress. Changing the law had been the point of the protests. Within a year Lyndon Johnson, who that November replaced Kennedy as president in the wake of his assassination, signed the Civil Rights Act; within two he'd signed the Voting Rights Act. But the shift from protesters' demands to congressional bills limited possibilities for radical transformation. Clear moral demands were replaced by horsetrading. Marchers cannot be stopped by a filibuster; legislation can.

"We were moving from a period of protest to one of political responsibility," said Rustin. "That is instead of marching on the courthouse, or the restaurant or the theater we now had to march the ballot box. In protest there must never be any compromise. In politics there is always compromise."

AS THE SOUTHERN CAUCUS'S RESPONSE to Kennedy's speech revealed, the nature of that deal-making was itself in flux. Veteran journalist Bill Moyers wrote that when the Civil Rights Act passed, Johnson was "euphoric." "But late that very night I found him in a melancholy mood as he lay in bed reading the bulldog edition of the *Washington Post* with headlines celebrating the day. I asked him what was troubling him. 'I think we just delivered the South to the Republican party for a long time to come,'" he said.

Johnson's fears were well founded: the Republicans, sensing an opportunity, decided to pitch a clear appeal to southern segregationists in particular and suburban white people in general on the grounds of race. This would create a fundamental realignment in the nation's politics that is only today beginning to unravel.

In 1964 the Republican presidential nominee, Arizona senator Barry Goldwater, opposed civil rights legislation and suffered crushing defeat. But by the next election the party of Lincoln had learned to be more subtle. In his diary, Richard Nixon's chief of staff Bob Haldeman describes how his boss spelled out the contours of the new electoral game plan: "You have to face the fact that the whole problem is really the blacks," Nixon told him. "The key is to devise a system that recognizes this while not appearing to."

The Republicans made appeals to racism that were both unmistakable and deniable, playing on racially loaded signs, signifiers, symbols, and metaphors, and would continue to do so for decades to come. Buffoonish proponents of outright segregation such as Bull Connor and George Wallace were replaced by those whose defense of white privilege was more nuanced and ostensibly dignified. Ronald Reagan demonized "welfare queens," a shorthand for Black women on welfare. George Bush Sr. made symbolic use of Willie Horton, the Black felon who committed assault, armed robbery, and rape while out of jail on a weekend furlough program approved by Bush's electoral opponent. Bush Jr. gave an address at Bob Jones University, an evangelical college that prohibited interracial dating into the twenty-first century.

"You start out in 1954 by saying, 'Nigger, nigger, nigger,'" explained the late Lee Atwater, one-time chair of the Republican National Committee and member of the Reagan administration, in 1981. "By 1968 you can't say 'nigger'—that hurts you. Backfires. So you say stuff like forced busing [and] states' rights.... You're getting so abstract now [that] you're talking about cutting taxes, and all these things you're talking about are totally economic things and a byproduct of them is [that] blacks get hurt worse than whites.... Obviously sitting around saying, 'We want to cut this,' is much more abstract than even the busing thing, and a hell of a lot more abstract than 'nigger, nigger.'"

For half a century it worked. From Reconstruction until 1964, Republicans had never won a majority of southern states. After 1964 they lost the former Confederacy only once, in 1976 to Jimmy Carter, who was from Georgia. Only in recent years with the rise of the Hispanic population and the emergence of a Black presidential candidate would this strategy require rethinking. "The demographics race we're losing badly," said Senator Lindsey Graham, ahead of the 2012 presidential election. "We're not generating enough angry white guys to stay in business for the long term."

Finally, there were the angry white men of the past. Evers's murder, and the subsequent failure to convict his assailant, illustrated the reign of terror that would pervade the South for many years to come. These crimes were not systematic: the manner in which they were carried out was far too crude for that. But they were systemic. They emerged from a system of segregation that could be sustained only through violence and implicit consent from the white population. While the perpetrators of racist murders were few in number, their crimes could not have occurred, or been covered up, without the tacit collusion of local power structures.

On the morning of September 15, 1963, just a fortnight after the March on Washington, fifteen-year-old Carolyn McKinstry went upstairs at the Sixteenth Street Baptist Church after Sunday school to hand in some papers to the office. She heard the phone ring. "When I answered it, the caller on the other end said, 'Three minutes,'" she told me. "As quickly as he said that, he hung up. I stepped out into the sanctuary and took about fifteen steps . . . when the bomb exploded."

Four young girls, Cynthia Wesley, Carole Robertson, and Addie Mae Collins, all fourteen, and eleven-year-old Denise McNair, died that morning. Even for many segregationists, murdering children in a church was an outrage.

Reflecting on King's speech and the historical moment in which it was delivered, Lewis later wrote: "There was no way we could have known then . . . that the hope and optimism contained in King's words would dwindle in the coming years, that in a matter of mere days after he stepped down from that stage a bomb blast in Birmingham would kill four little girls and usher in a season of darkness for the movement."

In the years that followed the march, the success of the civil rights movement created new challenges. The economic stratification of the Black community left it with a less cohesive base, while the political class's engagement with civil rights meant that the movement's leaders often found themselves eclipsed. In 1966 in Chicago, King could feel things slipping away. "I need some help in getting this method across. A lot of people have lost faith in the establishment. . . . They've lost faith in the democratic process. They've lost faith in non-violence," he said. Paraphrasing President Kennedy, he continued: "[T]hose who will make this peaceful revolution impossible will make a violent revolution inevitable, and we've got to get this over, I need help. I need some victories, I need concessions."

He would get precious few. In the part of his March on Washington speech where he refers to the nation's issuing "a bad check" to African Americans, he says: "We refuse to believe that there are insufficient funds in the great vaults of opportunity of this nation. And so we've come to cash this check, a check that will give us upon demand the riches of freedom and the security of justice." But for all the troubles following the passage of civil rights legislation, America was more comfortable dreaming about racial conviviality than dealing with racism's economic fallout and the redistributive policies needed to address it. Segregation may have eventually come to offend mainstream American sensibilities, but inequality per se did not. Indeed, at the heart of American mythology is the notion of class fluidity, social mobility, and personal reinvention, whereby inequality in wealth is acceptable as long as equality of opportunity is available. The fact that such equal opportunity was denied to Black citizens was not an issue with which most Americans were prepared to engage, so long as opportunity was not *explicitly* denied on grounds of race.

Rustin summed up the challenges in a much noted article in *Commentary* magazine in 1965 titled "From Protest to Power: The Future of the Civil Rights Movement":

> The civil rights movement is evolving from a protest movement into a full-fledged social movement—an evolution calling its very name into question. It is now concerned not merely with removing the barriers to full opportunity but with achieving the fact of equality. From sit-ins and freedom rides we have gone into rent strikes, boycotts, community organization, and political action. As a consequence of this natural evolution, the Negro today finds himself stymied by obstacles of far greater magnitude than the legal barriers he was attacking before: automation, urban decay, de facto school segregation. These are problems which, while conditioned by Jim Crow, do not vanish upon its demise. They are more deeply rooted in our socio-economic order; they are the result of the total society's failure to meet not only the Negro's needs, but human needs generally.

That's not to say that King made no effort to shift the terrain of the debate. In the years to come he would intersperse references to Mississippi with, for example, calls for justice for working-class whites in Appalachia. In this way he hoped to be seen as an advocate for the poor in general. He said in 1967:

This new phase is a struggle and a demand for genuine equality, and it is a much more difficult phase. It is much easier to integrate a lunch counter, for instance, then it is to eradicate slums. It is much easier to integrate buses than it is to create jobs. In the past in the civil rights movement we have been dealing with segregation and all of its humiliation. We've been dealing with the political problem of the denial of the right to vote. I think it is absolutely necessary now to deal massively and militantly with the economic problem. . . . So the grave problem facing us is the problem of economic deprivation, with the syndrome of bad housing and poor education and improper health facilities all surrounding this basic problem.

✦

SO KING'S "I Have a Dream" speech occurred at a pivotal moment. He was the most visible face of a demand—ending legal segregation—that seemed at the time not only plausible but inevitable. As long as the movement focused on that specific goal, all the protests, arrests, and even deaths that occurred along the way had a clear purpose; his speech, and the march at which it was delivered, reflected a general sense of optimism that things would change for the better.

However, once that struggle had been won the question of equality remained unanswered, leaving the coalition splintered and its aims either diluted or redirected to goals evidently much harder to attain and more difficult to define.

None of these developments happened immediately or evolved evenly. Far from it. King's star continued to ascend for a short time even as the fortunes of those he sought to lead waned. At the end of 1963 *Time* magazine named him Person of the Year; the following year he was awarded the Nobel Peace Prize. Meanwhile, on the ground, the movement continued to advance. The Mississippi Freedom Summer of 1964 registered swaths of new Black voters in the most racially hostile state of the Union. A year after that would be the Selma to Montgomery March in Alabama, demanding voting rights, and Johnson's commencement speech at the historically Black college Howard, in favor of affirmative action. Nonetheless, as the decade wore on, the mood of African Americans was increasingly infected with cynicism, despair, and even despondency.

At a meeting in Chicago in 1966, King was evidently shaken after being booed by young Black men in the crowd. He later recalled:

> I went home that night with an ugly feeling; selfishly I thought of my sufferings and sacrifices over the last twelve years. Why should they boo one so close to them? But as I lay awake thinking, I finally came to myself and I could not for the life of me have less than patience and understanding for those young people. For twelve years, I and others like me have held out radiant promises of progress, I had preached to them about my dream. . . . They were now hostile because they were watching the dream they had so readily accepted turn into a frustrating nightmare.

2

The March

"**SOMETIMES YOU JUST GET A SENSE** that the things you're in at the time are going to be historic," Joan Baez told me. "I remember looking out on Woodstock as I came down in a helicopter and knowing. And the march was kind of the same. As soon as you got there, you knew this was going to be a big one."

From the early morning of August 28, 1963, the Mall started filling up. By 9:30 a.m. forty thousand people had assembled; at 11:00 a.m. the number had more than doubled. By the time the march headed off, it had doubled again, and then more people joined until the crowd finally reached a quarter of a million—more than twice as many as the organizers had first hoped for. "What made the march was that Black people voted that day with their feet," said Bayard Rustin. "They came from every state, they came in jalopies, on trains, buses, anything they could get—some walked.

There were about three hundred congressmen there, but none of them said a word. We had told them to come, but we wanted to talk with them; they were not to talk to us."

White people made up around a fifth of the crowd, less than the organizers had expected. Clarence Jones was most impressed by the generational mix. "More surprising than the size of the crowd was its diversity in age. Naturally we had expected college students, even some high school students, but there were little children, septuagenarians, and everything in between. . . . That was an important key to the movement, out in the open but invisible to most who opposed us: it was never about me now, it was always about someone someday."

They poured onto the Mall, some singing, others listening to the entertainers performing from the steps of the Lincoln Memorial. Joan Baez ("We Shall Overcome" and "Oh Freedom"), Peter, Paul and Mary ("Blowin' in the Wind"), and Bob Dylan ("Only a Pawn in Their Game") kept the crowd entertained as it grew. By most accounts there was a raucous dignity to the occasion. Baez's most striking memory is looking out "at all the church hats." Writing in *Esquire* magazine, Norman Mailer recalled: "A deep blues went out from Washington in these hours: a revolutionary force existed in the land; it could move with violence, and it could move with discipline." William Geoghegan, the assistant deputy attorney general, viewed the day on a television in the Pentagon's war room, writes Euchner, and recalled: "When you see that crowd and the biracial content of it . . . I had to believe that it moved a lot of people and a lot of votes. It moved an awful lot of citizens who were very indifferent to realizing there's something that has to be done.

It had to have a powerful impact." There was "an electricity in the air," said Rustin. "Everyone who was there knew that the event was a landmark."

The historical importance of epoch-defining events like the March on Washington is rarely fully apparent at the time. It is only with the benefit of hindsight that they emerge as emblematic. Yet there was a broad consensus that day that something fundamental and consequential had occurred. Whatever ramifications the march might have for legislation or the movement, the very fact it had taken place, passed without violent incident, and been witnessed by millions was enough. "We've come here today to dramatize a shameful condition," King said in his speech. This was one act America was never going to forget.

Karl Marx wrote in *The Eighteenth Brumaire of Louis Bonaparte*:

> Men make their own history. But they do not make it as they please; they do not make it under self-selected circumstances, but under circumstances existing already, given and transmitted from the past. The tradition of all dead generations weighs like a nightmare on the brains of the living. And just as they seem to be occupied with revolutionizing themselves and things, creating something that did not exist before, precisely in such epochs of revolutionary crisis they anxiously conjure up the spirits of the past to their service, borrowing from them names, battle slogans, and costumes in order to present this new scene in world history in time-honored disguise and borrowed language.

So it was with the March on Washington, which was both bold in its conviction and old in its conception. Bold because national demonstrations in America's capital were rare at the time. "Marches on Washington have become ritualized dramas, carefully scripted and with few surprises," writes John D'Emilio in *Lost Prophet: The Life and Times of Bayard Rustin*. "In the decades [since the 1960s] virtually every cause, every constituency, every identity group has descended on the nation's capital, paraded through its streets, and assembled on the vast Mall to hear an array of speakers and entertainers. . . . This was not the case in 1963. Then the idea was . . . fresh and untried. No one had ever witnessed a mass descent on the nation's capital."

And it was old because the original idea for such a march had been hatched more than twenty years earlier, by the Black union and civil rights leader Asa Philip Randolph. In 1941 Randolph had called for a march on Washington against discrimination in the defense industry and segregation in the military. "The virtue and rightness of a cause are not alone the condition and cause of its progress and acceptance," he had argued when announcing the protest. "Power and pressure are at the foundation of the march of social justice and reform. . . . Power and pressure do not reside in the few, and the intelligentsia, they lie in and flow from the masses." The march was to be Black only. "There are some things Negroes must do alone," said Randolph. "This is our fight and we must see it through."

In *A. Philip Randolph: A Biographical Portrait*, Jervis Anderson relates how President Franklin Delano Roosevelt first tried to ignore Randolph's initiative. When the idea gathered steam, he called on his wife and other allies to persuade Randolph to call off the march, as he feared racial revolt at home ahead of a likely military conflict abroad. Randolph refused. Roosevelt then offered personally to call the armaments plants and order them to hire Blacks if the march was abandoned. Again Randolph refused. "We want you to do more than that. We want something concrete something tangible, definite, positive and affirmative," he insisted.

"Who the hell is this guy Randolph?" demanded Joseph Rauh, of the Office of Emergency Management, as Randolph rejected every draft he proposed on Roosevelt's behalf. "What the hell has he got over the president of the United States?"

A week before the march was scheduled to take place, Roosevelt blinked, issuing Executive Order 8802, which established a Fair Employment Practices Committee and effectively desegregated the war industries. It was only then that Randolph finally agreed to cancel the march, arguing that its objectives had been reached. While some in the movement condemned him for demobilizing so many, his standing grew as a result of the victory. "Randolph now became, and would remain for almost a decade, the most popular and sought-after black political figure in America," writes Anderson.

Now, in 1963, Randolph was at it again. While King may have been the most prominent civil rights leader at the time, Randolph, whom few Black people would have recognized by sight, was its most eminent. Born in Florida in 1889, Randolph became a union and civil rights leader, organizing the Brotherhood of Sleeping Car Porters, a union for the overwhelmingly African American staff on Pullman trains. Tall, dapper, and most often seen in dark woolen three-piece suits with a matching Homburg hat, he was also affectionately referred to as "St. Philip of the Pullman Porters" and "Black Messiah." "If he had been born in another time," noted John Lewis, "in another place or in another race, A. Philip Randolph would have been a prime minister or a president or a king." By the time of the March on Washington, he was seventy-four. This would be his last hurrah.

By his side, for both marches, was his long-standing ally and fellow socialist Bayard Rustin. twenty years his junior. Tall, eccentric, and intense, Rustin had salt-and-pepper hair that stood up in a short vertical mop, and his tie hung loose on his chest. Raised a Quaker, Rustin underwent a political development that would take him through pacifism, communism, and socialism and into the civil rights movement. In 1944, after refusing to fight in World War II, he had been jailed as a conscientious objector.

Rustin was also openly gay, an attribute that would mean that his contributions to a movement dominated by clerics were frequently marginalized. His position became particularly vulnerable following his arrest in Pasadena in 1953, when he was caught having sex with two men in a parked car. Charged with lewd vagrancy, he pled guilty to a lesser "morals charge." He was sent to jail for sixty days. By the time the march was proposed, writes D'Emilio, "he had recently turned fifty. He was still waiting for his day in the limelight, though likely believing it would never come. Prejudice of another sort, still not named as such in midcentury America, had curtailed his opportunities and limited his effectiveness."

And yet Rustin's exceptional abilities meant that, however uncomfortable his sexual orientation made others in the leadership of the movement feel, he became the key organizing figure behind the march. Whose idea it was to revive plans for a march after more than twenty years is not quite clear. It came up in December 1962 in Randolph's Harlem offices. But there was evidently less than a firm commitment to proceed at that time, since two months later Rustin took off to Dar es Salaam to work with the World Peace Brigade, promoting nonviolence in Africa's liberation struggles.

It wasn't until Rustin's return that planning got under way. With Black unemployment and racial income disparities high, the original idea was to focus the demands of the march at least as much on issues of economics as on those of discrimination. Rustin initially envisaged a two-day event. On the first day there would be "a mass descent" on the Capitol with the intention of overwhelming representatives with such "a staggering series of labor, church, civil rights delegations from their own states that they would be unable to conduct business on the floor of Congress." On the second day there would be "a mass protest rally [that] would project our concrete 'Emancipation Proclamation' to the nation."

Initially the response was lukewarm. Whitney Young of the National Urban League declined to have anything to do with it, believing his participation might hamper his lobbying work and even imperil the nonprofit tax status of the league. Roy Wilkins, the head of the NAACP, who considered legal and legislative pressure to be of greater value than direct action and civil disobedience, was too busy organizing a conference at which President Kennedy would be a keynote speaker. King was ambivalent. The previous year he had been keen to use 1963 to leverage the symbolic value of the centenary of the Emancipation Proclamation, when Lincoln decreed all slaves in the Confederacy free, but his appeals to Kennedy on that score had come to nothing.

Most supportive of the idea of the march were the organizations on the frontline of the struggle: the Congress of Racial Equality (CORE) and the Student Non-Violent Co-ordinating Committee

(SNCC). Both had large activist bases North and South, including a significant proportion of youth. But even their enthusiasm was qualified. SNCC was more committed to bringing to the streets of the nation's capital the dynamism of its direct action that had so effectively challenged segregation in the Deep South. "The feeling among most of the rank and file of SNCC was that if we did take part in this march, we should do it our way, which would be to turn this demonstration into a protest rather than a plea," explains John Lewis, who was SNCC's chair at the time. "Stage sit-ins all across Washington. Tie up traffic. Have 'lie-ins' on local airport runways. Invade the offices of southern congressmen and senators. Camp on the White House lawn. Cause mass arrests. Paralyze the city."

Given the original reticence of the NACCP, the Urban League, and King regarding this kind of protest, the likelihood of the march's turning out this way seemed improbable. Indeed, at this stage the entire enterprise was looking unlikely. Then along came Birmingham. The sight of children being bludgeoned, hosed, and hounded shifted both national awareness and the political calculus of what was both possible and necessary for the civil rights movement.

Signing on to a national demonstration now posed less of a risk to the credibility of Wilkins, Young, and their organizations than steering clear of it. The march was clearly going ahead whether they supported it or not. They could either put themselves at the head of it or be left trailing behind it. "Birmingham became the moment of truth," declared Rustin. "Birmingham meant that 'tokenism is finished.'"

By early June, King was sounding enthusiastic about the march— he had almost convinced himself that it was his own idea. "We are on the threshold of a significant breakthrough and the greatest weapon is a mass demonstration," he told his aides. "We are at the point where we can mobilize all this righteous indignation into a powerful mass movement."

Rustin and Randolph had to move fast to capitalize on the opening Birmingham had provided. Randolph convened an emergency meeting of the main civil rights leaders: King, Young, Wilkins, Lewis, and James Farmer, the head of CORE. Meanwhile Rustin reoriented the demonstration to better reflect the demands of the new situation. It was now to be the March for Jobs and Freedom. The activity that had previously been planned to take place over two days, including a march, congressional lobbying, and demonstrations at the Capitol and the White House, was now to be compressed into one.

If the more conservative elements of the movement felt that post-Birmingham they had little choice but to be associated with the demonstration, the more moderate sectors of Washington's political class felt they had little choice but to disown it and, if possible, prevent it from happening.

The Kennedy administration was jittery. "Everyone started getting panicky," recalled Burke Marshall. "People down on the Hill particularly thought it was going to be terrible." The fear was partly about the possibility of violence. To the political elite, convinced that power resided only within their hallowed walls, a march was not so much an act of protest as acting out. Charles Diggs, a Black congressman from Detroit, told King about his "increasing concern" regarding a march. "I am sure a graceful withdrawal could be conceived," he urged.

But popular consciousness was moving faster than conventional wisdom could fathom. Politics, any gradualist, reformer, or career politician will inform you, is "the art of the possible." That's as true as it is axiomatic. But politics is also about having the courage to imagine new possibilities and developing the wherewithal to make them materialize. "What can we do today so that we can do tomorrow what we cannot do today?"—as the socialist educator Paulo Freire once put it. In the spring and summer of 1963 each day brought new possibilities that made feasible tomorrow what had been unthinkable only yesterday. Such was the momentum that elevated the march from a political orphan to the child of many parents.

✦

WHILE THE WHITE HOUSE was slow to grasp the depth of the crisis, and consequently unable to acknowledge the potential magnitude of the march, by midsummer it was forced to face the march's impending arrival head on. The president's televised address on June 11, when he had pledged to introduce legislation, meant his administration was caught up in this fight regardless. On June 22 Kennedy finally met with civil rights leaders to discuss the march.

Before the meeting Kennedy invited King for a private conversation in the Rose Garden, where he insisted that King purge "communists" that the president insisted, were secretly working in the movement on behalf of a foreign power. King protested, Kennedy insisted, and then they headed for the Cabinet Room, where they were joined by Randolph, Wilkins, Farmer, Lewis, and Young, among others.

The president's brother Bobby sat silently in a corner of the room, a daughter on his knee, as Kennedy shook hands briskly with each of the leaders before explaining his political vulnerabilities. Since his civil rights address, his favorability ratings had plummeted from 60 to 47 percent. "I may lose the next election because of this," he said.

Wilkins expressed the group's support for Kennedy's civil rights bill before Young asked him directly whether he backed the march. Kennedy said he didn't. "We want success in Congress, not just a big show at the Capitol. Some of these people are looking for an excuse to be against us. I don't want to give any of them a chance to say, 'Yes, I'm for the bill, but I'm damned if I will vote for it at the point of a gun.' It seemed to me a great mistake to announce a march on Washington before the bill was even in committee. The only effect is to create an atmosphere of intimidation—and this may give some members of Congress an out."

Randolph had been through this before, with FDR, and was not about to let the opportunity of a huge protest slip away for the vague promise of incremental gain. In any case, as he explained to Kennedy, those assembled in the Cabinet Room weren't leading, they were following. "The Negroes are already in the streets, and it is very likely impossible to get them off," he said. "If they are bound to be in the streets in any case, is it not better that they be led by organizations dedicated to civil rights and disciplined by struggle rather than to leave them to other leaders who care neither about civil rights nor about nonviolence? If the civil rights leadership were to call the Negroes off the streets, it is problematic whether they would come."

It was a telling exchange. The Kennedys feared violence if the march took place; Randolph feared violence if it didn't. But both the White House and the civil rights leaders effectively conceded that they were not fully in control of events and were now discussing their respective responsibilities for managing the frustrations that were percolating through Black America.

While Kennedy had made it clear that he preferred no march at all, he was aware that if it was going ahead anyway it would be better for him if it passed peacefully and was not centered on demands that were incompatible with his legislative efforts. Most of the civil rights leaders were eager for his support and, for their own credibility, needed the march to be nonviolent. To that extent the two sides had a shared interest.

King, who had hitherto deferred to Randolph's age, experience, and stature during the White House meeting, chimed in toward the end with a précis of the letter he had written from his Birmingham prison cell. "It may seem ill-timed. Frankly, I have never engaged in a direct-action movement that did not seem ill-timed. Some people thought Birmingham was ill-timed."

"Including the attorney general," joked the president. "I don't think you should all be totally harsh on Bull Connor," he continued lightheartedly. "After all, he has done more for civil rights than almost anybody else."

Lewis recalls, "The talk went back and forth in a generally pleasant way. . . . When Wilkins noted that we would have problems with our own organizations and memberships if we did not march, the president stood up, sighed, and said, 'Well, we all have our problems. You have your problems. I have my problems.'" With that he rushed off to his final briefing for his impending trip to Europe, leaving the impression that he would not publicly oppose the march even if he thought it unwise.

✦

TEN DAYS LATER the six main civil rights leaders, Young, Wilkins, Farmer, King, Lewis, and Randolph, met again, this time at the Roosevelt Hotel in Harlem. The purpose of this meeting was to hammer out the ground rules under which they would work together. The atmosphere was cordial until Wilkins arrived. "Wilkins was really asserting himself," Lewis writes. "The moment [he] entered the room he came across to me as some sort of New Yorker who thought he was smarter than the rest of the group. He seemed to feel that King was basically a careless, unsophisticated country preacher and to envy the power and position Dr. King had attained." Unhappy with the large entourages some leaders had brought with them, Wilkins cavalierly winnowed the meeting's attendees down to the bare minimum, tapping people on the shoulder and declaring: "This one goes, this one stays, this one goes."

His main issue that day was Rustin, whose political and sexual transgressions, argued Wilkins, made him a liability. "I don't want you leading that march on Washington, because you know I don't give a damn about what they say, but publicly I don't want to have to defend the draft dodging," he said. "I know you're a Quaker, but that's not what I'll have to defend. I'll have to defend draft dodging. I'll have to defend promiscuity. The question is never going to be homosexuality, it's going to be promiscuity and I can't defend that.

And the fact is that you were a member of the Young Communist League. And I don't care what you say, I can't defend that."

While Wilkins's manner may have been abrasive, his concerns were standard at the time. Farmer, shortly before he died, explained to me how he vetted people for the Freedom Rides in 1961. "We had to screen them very carefully because we knew that if they found anything to throw at us, they would throw it. We checked for communists, homosexuals, drug addicts. . . . I personally interviewed people and then would talk to their friends."

Not much had changed in the intervening years. Rustin was indeed vulnerable on many counts, but he had many strengths too. He had built strong relationships with most of those in the room, and they knew his organizational talents to be beyond doubt. With a mere two months before the demonstration was to take place, his personal vulnerabilities were not the sole pragmatic concern.

Randolph technically agreed to Wilkins's demand, only to then outmaneuver him. "I will take on [being leader] of the March under one circumstance," he told the group. "And that is that I will be free to choose my own deputy, and my deputy is going to be Bayard Rustin."

Wilkins grudgingly conceded. "You can take that on if you want. But don't expect me to do anything about it when the trouble starts."

The following eight weeks, writes D'Emilio,

> were the busiest in Rustin's life. He had to build an organization out of nothing. He had to assemble a staff and shape them into a team able to perform under intense pressure. He had to craft a coalition that would hang together despite organizational competition, personal animosities, and often antagonistic

politics. He had to maneuver through the minefield of an opposition that ranged from liberals who were counseling moderation to segregationists out to sabotage the event. And he had to do all of this while staying enough out of the public eye so that the liabilities he carried would not undermine his work.

The headquarters for this extraordinary endeavor was a rented run-down former church on West 130th and Lenox in Harlem. A banner was draped above its entrance declaring, "National Headquarters: March on Washington for Jobs and Freedom: Wed, AUG 28th." The building soon resembled a cross between a student union in occupation and a military headquarters on high alert.

"It was very exciting and frenetic," Rachelle Horowitz, the march's transport chief, who was also Rustin's longtime assistant, told me. "It ran on adrenaline and excitement with everybody working from early in the morning till late into the night. It was very collegial, very primitive, and very egalitarian."

"Visitors," writes Anderson, "found it hard to believe that an enterprise of such proportions was being planned amid such humble appointments in an office furnished with nothing more than a water cooler, a few scabrous and creaky old desks and chairs, and a small bank of temporary telephones. Assisted by a handful of Black and white volunteers, Rustin prepared thousands of letters, instruction manuals and newsletters."

"I think the mood could best be described . . . as one of gaiety," wrote Harvey Swados in *The Nation* magazine. "This élan, this sense of participation in something that grew even as they planned for it, as with parents who discuss the future of their child while he sleeps."

It was a tribute to Rustin's eccentric, hyperactive, and efficient personality. He was in constant motion, interrupting conversations to answer phones even as he passed notes to staff, doodled, and chain-smoked. "I had had many differences with Bayard in the past and was destined to have more differences with him in the future," recalled Farmer. "But I must say that I have never seen such a difficult task of coordination performed with more skill and deftness."

"He wanted us to live that couple of months as if every single day might be the last day of your life," recalls Norman Hill, a CORE field director who had been seconded to help organize the march. "You had to accomplish as much as possible every day."

The entire time Rustin, a compulsive list maker, would be writing down tasks, crossing them off, and writing down more. He worked on the principle that anything that could go wrong would. Euchner describes how before people left for home each day, a staff meeting was held where everyone would relate what had they'd achieved. Rustin had once been a professional singer. "Sometimes, like a herald from the past, Rustin suddenly interrupted the chatter with an old spiritual, his voice sweet and high pitched: *Sometimes I feel like a motherless child / A long ways from home / A true believer.*"

The planning was both meticulous and basic. "We wanted to get everybody from the whole country into Washington by nine o'-clock in the morning and out of Washington by sundown," said Rustin. "This required all kinds of things that you had to think through. We planned out precisely the number of toilets that would be needed for a quarter of a million people, how many blankets we would need for the people who were coming in early, . . . how many doctors, how many first aid stations, what people should bring with them to eat in their lunches. . . . We had of course to have fantastic planning of all the parking lots for the thousands of buses and automobiles. We anticipated all problems." They advised people not to put mayonnaise in their sandwiches, for example, because it spoils easily in the sun and can cause diarrhea.

The blend of functionality and ambition was exemplified in Rustin's demands for a sound system. When ordering the system, he told engineers: "The Lincoln Memorial is here, the Washington Monument is there. I want one square mile where anyone can hear." As he explained later: "In my view it was a classic resolution of the problem of how can you keep a crowd from becoming something else. Transform it into an audience." The system he decided was needed cost ten times as much as his meager budget permitted. But with the help of union donations, he got it anyway.

By the end of July the hard work was clearly paying off. The civil rights establishment was on board and mobilizing its supporters, giving Randolph both the confidence and the authority to broaden the coalition by inviting religious groups. Trade unions were central to the effort. Unions representing those working in the electrical, fur, auto, packing, garment, transport, municipal, and retail sectors were all represented, as were those of Catholic, Jewish, and Protestant faiths. By the end of July, Catholic activists were galvanizing the flock, unions were booking buses, and, Hollywood to New York, celebrities were signing up to attend.

In these last few weeks, the march organizers felt they were on the brink of something huge. "Caution turned to excitement," writes D'Emilio, "worry to anticipation, as evidence accumulated that the size of the march was likely to surpass anyone's wildest dreams."

When Rustin had written to every member of Congress earlier in the summer, many had made excuses. Now, sensing the shifting mood, they too started attaching themselves to the event. Rustin later recalled: "As we got closer [and they] saw it was going to be bigger and more important, the relatives became less important, the trips home became less important, the going to Europe became less important."

In their caution politicians were merely channeling the broader electorate's division and discomfort. For while the march now promised to be big, it was by no means popular. A Gallup poll just a few weeks before it took place revealed that 71 percent of Americans were familiar with "the proposed mass civil rights rally to be held in Washington, D.C., on August 28." And of those who were familiar, 23 percent had a favorable view, 42 percent had an unfavorable view, 18 percent thought it wouldn't accomplish anything, and 7 percent predicted that there would be violence.

"Some of the civil rights leaders were worried at first, because many sympathetic people in Congress and the White House worried that if violence broke out at the march, it could hold back civil rights legislation," explains Horowitz. "So their friends were saying: 'Don't do this. It could cause more problems than it will help.' It took time to galvanize all these forces to say 'We'll do it.'"

As the coalition supporting the march grew, so the leaders' appetite for more militant proposals for the event, like disrupting traffic and mass civil disobedience, diminished. Among other things, they abandoned plans to give a prominent speaker's slot to an unemployed worker and to march around the White House.

Back in Harlem, each time Rustin announced that yet another

radical element had been dropped, his young staff would berate him, part in jest, part in frustration. "We'd shout: 'Oh Bayard, you're turning it into a circus!'" Horowitz told me with a laugh. Vincent Harding, an activist and close friend of King's at the time, did not make the trip. "There was a certain hard-headedness among some of us at the time," he explained to me. "We were interested in a March *on* Washington. When it became a March *in* Washington, we lost interest." Andrew Young, one of King's closest aides, told me he had not intended to go because he assumed it would be "a huge picnic." "Many of us who had been active that year thought it was an opportunity to rest." He only attended after King called and persuaded him that he "didn't want to miss this one."

Ever the coalition builder, Rustin explained: "What you have to understand is that the march will succeed if it gets a hundred thousand people—or 150,000 or 200,000 or more—to show up in Washington. It will be the biggest rally in history. It will show the Black community united as never before—united also with whites from labor and the churches, from all over the country."

The principal reason that most of the more militant tactics were dropped was security. From the moment the march was announced, this was always the primary concern of the administration and a considerable worry for the organizers. These concerns were partly rooted in logistics. A march of this size was unprecedented in Washington, a southern and deeply segregated city. Furthermore, it was being brought together quickly and on a tight budget.

The anxieties were also shaped by strategic considerations. The march was coming at the end of a tumultuous summer of violent racial conflict, during which frustration with the slow pace of change had exhausted the patience of many Black Americans. Scenes in Birmingham and elsewhere had shown that the tenets of nonviolence on which the civil rights movement had been built were not shared by all of its followers, particularly when they were provoked by racists, in or out of uniform. There was a risk, in short, that the sort of chaos and bloodshed experienced in the South might be imported to the capital, but on a far bigger scale.

But the overwhelming cause of worries about violence was grounded in racism. The way the media and politicians described it, hundreds of thousands of angry Black people bringing their base ways, impulsive manners, and uncivilized mores to confront power could only end in chaos and calamity. No hyperbole, it seemed, was too inflated.

On the Monday before the march, South Carolina representative William Dorn warned that it imperiled nothing less than the future of democracy and the security of the republic: "Mr. Speaker, . . . the march on Washington this week will set a dangerous precedent. It is reminiscent of the Mussolini Fascist blackshirt march on Rome in 1922. It is reminiscent of the Socialist Hitler's government-sponsored rallies in Nuremberg." One newspaper cartoon depicted African Americans marching toward a powder keg marked "Washington D.C."

✦

PANIC MEASURES WERE IN FULL FORCE. It was as though the city were under siege. All elective surgeries were canceled; sales of alcohol in the capital were banned; the Washington Senators, the local baseball team, postponed their games; senators told their female staff to stay home; Chief Judge John Lewis Smith Jr. of the District of Columbia Court of General Sessions warned his fifteen colleagues to be prepared for criminal hearings to run through the night.

Fearing incitement from the podium, the Justice Department secretly inserted a cutoff switch in the sound system so they could turn off the speakers if an insurgent group hijacked the microphone. In such an eventuality, the plan was to play a recording of Mahalia Jackson singing "He's Got the Whole World in His Hands" in order to calm down the crowd. *Life* magazine reported: "Merely contemplating the possibilities for trouble and the logistics of the demonstration has given Washington officialdom its worst case of invasion jitters since the First Battle of Bull Run."

Between them the Pentagon, the White House, the Justice Department, and the DC police force turned the policing of the march into a military operation. It was codenamed Operation Steep Hill. Euchner details how one thousand troops and thirty helicopters were deployed in the DC area. The Pentagon put nineteen thousand troops on standby. The Eighty-Second Airborne Division, based in Fort Bragg, North Carolina, stood by with C-82 "flying boxcars" loaded with guns, ammunition, and food, ready at a moment's notice to make the 320-mile trip to Andrews Air Force Base in Maryland, from which soldiers would be dispatched to the Mall by helicopter to quell riots. Around six thousand law-enforcement officers of different kinds would be deployed that day (with another four thousand in the vicinity awaiting orders), all armed with guns, clubs, and tear gas. The one concession to civil rights sensitivities was that there would be no dogs.

Given the nature of previous social disturbances connected with the civil rights movement, these measures were both overblown and counterintuitive. As Rustin pointed out at a meeting with Justice Department officials in mid-July, Black people had rarely been the source of violent unrest. "Historically groups of Negroes have no history of creating violence in their demonstrations," he told them. "Violence usually has been created by agents outside the Negro protest and very often in the South by police."

As far as the state was concerned, the only public-safety issue that merited attention was Black unrest. Rustin asked the Justice Department whether marchers coming from around the country could expect protection against racists. "Suppose Negroes from Mississippi are coming in a busload, and the buses are attacked and burned— say, the night before the march. Then the meeting will take place in an entirely different psychological atmosphere." The Justice Department declined to take action to prevent attacks of this kind.

It was at this point that the contradictions inherent in the collaboration between the government, the state, and the march organizers became bizarre. They were working together, but not as equals. And they were working against each other, but rarely openly. The FBI was tapping the phones of King and his most trusted aides. The government helped Rustin procure a speaker system at the last minute, after the one he got was sabotaged, but did not disclose the breaker switch it had inserted. Rustin allowed a Justice Department official to assist the organizing committee, only to complain afterward that he "almost smothered us. We had to keep raising our demands to keep him from getting ahead of us." In one particularly comic example, Euchner points out, a civil rights worker trained volunteers in how to manage conflict and emphasized the possibility of agents provocateurs from the FBI. It later turned out that he himself was a paid informant for the FBI.

The movement itself had a much more nuanced approach to security matters than the government and police force. Fearing that troops of armed white police flanking a mostly Black march would send the wrong signal, Rustin decided that the demonstration should be, first and foremost, self-policed. He recruited William Johnson, a retired police officer, to bring together more than a thousand active and retired policemen to form the Guardians. The aim was to keep discipline in the march with a light touch. If tensions mounted, they were instructed to lead the crowd in singing "We Shall Overcome."

In the meantime, the veracity of Rustin's maxim that anything that could go wrong would go wrong was repeatedly proved. Segregationist senator Strom Thurmond took to the Senate floor to brand Rustin a "Communist, draft-dodger and homosexual," entering into the congressional record a picture of Rustin talking to King while King was in a bathtub. But the attack came too late and from too poisoned a well to have any impact beyond rallying support for Rustin. "I'm sure there were some homophobes in the movement," said activist Eleanor Holmes. "But you knew how to behave when Strom Thurmond attacked."

Meanwhile, the chauvinism of a movement dominated by males while supported by many women in its ranks was challenged after it transpired that not a single woman would be allowed to take the microphone on the day unless she was singing. Some of the movement's central figures, including Rosa Parks, Septima Clark, Ella Baker, Daisy Bates, and Diane Nash, were not allowed to march alongside the men. Coretta Scott King and other wives were also diverted to a separate procession on Independence Avenue.

Black activist and educator Anna Hedgeman was particularly incensed and challenged the march organizers over the gender imbalance on the platform. She confronted Horowitz in the lobby of the Statler Hotel. "What are you going to do about the women?" she asked. "You are betraying the cause of women if you go along with this."

Eleanor Holmes, also Black, walked by. "Philip Randolph represents me," she said.

"You too have betrayed me and all womanhood," insisted Hedgeman.

To crown this catalog of calamities, it turned out that James Farmer, one of the march's key organizers, was stuck in jail in Louisiana. A week earlier Farmer had led a march in downtown Plaquemine protesting police brutality. He was arrested, along with local leaders and more than two hundred activists. Bail was set at five hundred dollars, and with the jails in Plaquemine full, Farmer was transferred, along with some others, to nearby Donaldsonville.

CORE did not have enough money to bail out everybody, and with the march approaching the organization's leaders had to come to a decision: Should they arrange the release of their leader so that he could address the biggest march in civil rights history and reach a global audience? Or should they maintain a principled position of keeping close to their base and leave Farmer in jail along with the rank-and-file members of the movement?

They decided to resist significant pressure from the march organizers and keep Farmer where he was. "We decided at CORE that we would make a better statement with Jim in jail than at the March on Washington," Lolis Edward Elie, the group's lawyer, told Charles Euchner. "Anybody with an ounce of ego would want to be in Washington.... [Jim] wanted to be there. But the group made that decision not to be there." Rudy Lombard, leader of CORE's Louisiana campaign, added: "We would not ask the local people to do anything that the CORE representatives would not do. That would apply to all of us, including Jim. We didn't think that going to Washington and participating in the march was any more important than staying involved with the community."

✦

ON THE EVE OF THE MARCH, a sticking point emerged that threatened to derail the entire event. It would run like an open sore into the next day, even as the demonstration was under way. Lewis arrived back to his hotel room at around 2:00 that morning to find a handwritten note under his door.

"John. Come downstairs. Must see you at once. Bayard."

No sooner had he read it than the phone rang.

"We've got a problem," said Rustin.

"A problem. What problem?" said Lewis

"It's your speech. Some people are very concerned about some of the things you're going to say in your speech. You need to get down here. We need to talk."

Lewis' speech was, if nothing else, faithful to the spirit of militancy and frustration that was taking over the movement. It reflected the mood that the established civil rights organizations were struggling to keep up with. That, in no small part, was why it attracted so much hostility from the other leaders. The speech described Kennedy's civil rights bill as "too little and too late." Echoing King's *Letter from Birmingham Jail*, Lewis derided the call for patience. "We cannot be patient, we do not want to be free gradually. We want our freedom, and we want it *now*." And in his most inflammatory metaphor, envoking General Sherman's Civil War march to the sea, which left much of the former Confederacy destroyed, he planned to say, "We will march through the South, through the heart of Dixie, the way Sherman did. We shall pursue our own 'scorched earth' policy and burn Jim Crow to the ground—nonviolently."

The day before, a SNCC staffer had seen copies of other speeches on a table in the foyer of the Statler Hotel and, fearing that coverage of SNCC's contribution to the march would be eclipsed, ordered Lewis's speech to be placed on the table as well.

Copies circulated quickly, and so did the controversy. When the speech was seen by Walter Reuther, the leader of the United Automobile Workers, a major backer of the march, he was immediately alarmed and called Wilkins. He said he'd seen it too and agreed it was a problem. Reuther then took it to King, who was also deeply concerned. "Well, John Lewis can't make that speech," King said. "This is completely contrary to everything we are doing."

The person most incensed was Washington's Archbishop Patrick O'Boyle, who was scheduled to deliver the march's invocation. He called the White House to complain and then rang Rustin to warn him that he would pull out of the event if Lewis was allowed to deliver his prepared text.

In his autobiography Lewis recalls that when he arrived at Rustin's room, Rustin seemed calm. The main sticking point for O'Boyle, Rustin told him, was Lewis's eschewing of patience.

"This is offensive to the Catholic Church," explained Rustin.

"Why?"

"Payyyy .... tience ... Catholics *believe* in the word 'patience.'"

Rustin warned this wasn't the last complaint Lewis would hear about the proposed speech but suggested they postponed further discussions so they could all get some sleep. "We had a big day ahead of us," he told Lewis.

"By the time I got back to my room I was incensed," wrote Lewis. "This was a good speech. Maybe a great one. That's how everyone who had seen it felt—everyone with SNCC.... I had told Bayard I would listen to the others the next day, but I made no promises. And the more I thought about it as I fell asleep that night ... the less inclined I was to change one word."

At breakfast the following morning, none of the leaders made reference to Lewis's speech. But as the day progressed, negotiations over the metaphors within it themselves became metaphors for the deeper divisions within the movement.

Rustin saw some parts of the speech as at odds with one of the march's principal aims: building critical support for Kennedy's bill. O'Boyle was worried about more conservative members of the church and his relationship with the Kennedys. SNCC, meanwhile, was concerned about maintaining its credibility with its base in the Deep South.

✦

EUCHNER DESCRIBES HOW for several days people had been making their way to Washington however they could. Buses left California to travel several thousand miles. The night before in Savannah, a chartered train left with its passengers singing "We Shall Overcome." Ledger Smith, a twenty-seven-year-old truck driver, roller-skated seven hundred miles from Chicago wearing a sash saying "FREEDOM"; an eighty-two-year-old cycled from Ohio; a young man cycled from North Dakota. Horowitz persuaded New York's Metropolitan Transport Authority to keep the subways running overnight on a rush-hour schedule so New Yorkers could get to their buses, while bridge and tunnel authorities handed out leaflets from their booths containing information about the march.

Few had made it to the Mall shortly after dawn, leading some news reporters to predict the whole enterprise would be a flop. But as the morning progressed, evidence that the weeks of organizing had borne fruit began to emerge on the streets of DC. "By 9:00 or 10:00 that morning we knew it would be a great success," says Horowitz. Twenty-one charter trains came into Union Station along with many scheduled services carrying mainly protesters. A human deluge poured into the city from every part of the country. By midday roughly forty charters had brought in twenty thousand riders, who were then taken to the Washington Monument by shuttle.

Media interest in the march was intense. "The Metropolitan Police Department handled more press requests than it ever had," wrote Gene Roberts and Hank Klibanoff in *The Race Beat: The Press, the Civil Rights Struggle and the Awakening of a Nation*. "By 1963 standards the coverage was saturation. On NBC the *Today Show* devoted more than thirty minutes to the march. The network then aired eleven special reports during the day, totaling more than three hours of coverage. . . . One special report on Martin Luther King's appearance went for an hour. The network ended with a forty-five-minute show late that night. ABC also inserted special reports throughout the day."

The Mall was awash with Hollywood celebrities, many convened by Ossie Davis. They flew in from Los Angeles in two chartered planes. Charlton Heston, Sidney Poitier, Billy Wilder, Tony Curtis, Sammy Davis Jr., Burt Lancaster, James Garner, and Harry Belafonte were there. Marlon Brando wandered around brandishing an electric cattle prod, a symbol of police brutality. Josephine Baker made it over from France; Paul Newman abandoned the celebrity section to mix with the crowd. Julian Bond, a young SNCC activist who would one day become the chairman of the NAACP, was charged with plying the stars with Coca-Cola.

Many of the celebrities had received calls from FBI agents the night before or that morning urging them to remain in their hotels to avoid the violence they claimed was bound to occur. George Rockwell, leader of the US Nazi Party, had vowed to bring ten thousand white supremacists to protest the march. Just over seventy showed up.

That morning the civil rights leaders met with congressional representatives to discuss the issues raised by the demonstration. Lewis described the meetings as "quick cordial sessions. Nothing substantial, simply courtesy calls arranged early in the morning so we would have plenty of time to make it over to the Lincoln Memorial for the beginning of the event."

The restless and excited crowd, however, proved irrepressible. While the leaders were chatting with the politicians, the masses started the march without them. The symbolism was not lost on Rustin.

"My God, they're *going*. We're supposed to be leading *them*," he said.

Loudspeakers called for them to stop, but no one listened.

"My first impulse was to try and stop it and wait for the leaders," said Rustin. "But I figured I was going to get run over. I'd better get the hell out of there, and I left."

The marchers had left early. When the leaders came out of the meetings, they jumped into waiting black limousines and tried to catch up. But they got stuck in traffic—the traffic created by the march. Abandoning the cars, they leaped out on Constitution Avenue, locked arms, and waded into the middle of the procession.

"Photos ran in newspapers the next day as if we were in front of the march," wrote Lewis. "But we couldn't even see the front. As people turned and recognized us, they began clearing the way and sweeping us along from behind, and that's how we came to the Lincoln Memorial, the leaders being pushed along by the people—as it should be."

Meanwhile the dispute over Lewis's speech was intensifying. Reuther called O'Boyle, who said he had a statement signed by thirteen bishops dissociating themselves from the march. Reuther asked him to hold back the statement for half an hour so that he could present an ultimatum to the coalition. "Look, we have got a decision to make real quick, and there is no use debating it because we haven't got time. . . . If John Lewis feels strongly that he wants to make this speech, he can go someplace else and make it, but he has no right to make it here because if he tries to make it he destroys the integrity of our coalition and he drives people out of the coalition who agree to the principles. . . . This is just immoral and he has no right to do it, and I demand a vote right now because I have got to call the archbishop."

Reuther got his way. Rustin convened an impromptu committee comprising King, Randolph, Rustin, Carson Blake of the National Council of Churches, and Lewis to find a solution. They met in a security guard's office beneath Lincoln's statue. Reuther called O'Boyle: "Your Excellency, I think we have solved your problem and ours too. We have set up this subcommittee. If they agree that the speech complies, then John Lewis will make the speech. If they agree that it doesn't, he will be denied the floor." Then Randolph and Blake confirmed to O'Boyle that they had agreed to the arrangement.

The music was winding up; the speeches were about to begin. After Marian Anderson sang the national anthem, Boyle gave the invocation on the basis of Reuther's promise. That meant a resolution had to be reached. The exclusion of Lewis would be a problem for SNCC. But given SNCC's grassroots credentials and leadership on the frontline, not to mention Farmer's absence, it would also be a problem for the march.

The controversy was becoming increasingly bitter. Wilkins accused Lewis of "double-crossing the people who had gathered to support this bill."

Lewis retorted: "I'm speaking for my colleagues in SNCC and for the people in the Delta and in the Black Belt. You haven't been there, Mr. Wilkins. You don't understand."

Up on stage Rustin delivered a tribute to "Negro women fighters for freedom." Rosa Parks, Daisy Bates, Prince E. Lee, Diane Nash, and Gloria Richardson were called on to take a bow and say not a word. Nash, listening to the event on the radio (she had decided to rest rather than attend the march), was surprised to hear her name called.

Back below the monument the debate over Lewis's speech continued unabated. Lewis was next on the podium. King expressed avuncular disappointment at his reference to Sherman. "I know you, John," he said, "and that doesn't sound like you."

"It looked as if no one was going to budge," wrote Lewis. "Then Randolph stepped in. He looked beaten down and very tired."

"I have waited twenty-two years for this," said Randolph. "I've waited all my life for this opportunity. Please don't ruin it. John, we've come this far together. Let us stay together."

His entreaty melted Lewis's resolve. "He looked as if he might cry. This was as close to a plea as a man as dignified as he could come. How could I say no? It would be like saying no to Mother Teresa. I said I would fix it."

Lewis's speech had openly questioned Kennedy's commitment to civil rights and lambasted the legislation he was proposing in particular and the political class in general. Line by line, some of his most scathing criticisms and inflammatory metaphors were stripped away. Lewis took out the parts about the bill being "too little and too late" and "[marching] through the heart of Dixie the way Sherman did." The question "Which side is the federal government on?" was also deleted, as was the word "cheap" to describe some political leaders. "I was angry," said Lewis. "But when we were done, I was satisfied. . . . The speech still had fire. It still had bite. . . . It still had an edge."

✦

OF ALL THE SPEECHES that day, Lewis's did indeed stand out. Randolph had opened the program with the words: "Fellow Americans, we are gathered here in the largest demonstration in the history of this nation. Let the nation and the world know the meaning of our numbers. We are not a pressure group, we are not an organization or a group of organizations, we are not a mob. We are the advance guard of a massive moral revolution for jobs and freedom."

On the morning of the march, news had arrived from Africa that one of the country's great Black intellectuals and activists, W. E. B. Du Bois, had died. Du Bois had been living in Ghana, where he had vowed to play his part in building a new continent. His passing was announced by Wilkins from the podium. "If you want to read something that applies to 1963, go back and get a volume of *The Souls of Black Folk* by Du Bois, published in 1903," he said. The opening line of the second chapter states: "The problem of the twentieth century is the problem of the color line."

Reverend Blake spoke to the whites in the crowd: "We come—late, late we come—in the reconciling and repentant spirit" of Lincoln.

Reuther spoke without a script. Referring to Kennedy's recent appearance at the Brandenburg Gate, he said: "We cannot defend freedom in Berlin so long as we deny freedom in Birmingham."

Recalling his time as a rabbi in Berlin under Hitler, Rabbi Joachim Prinz said: "A great people who had created a great civilization had become a nation of silent onlookers. They remained silent in the face of hate, in the face of brutality, and in the face of mass murder. . . . America must not become a nation of onlookers. America must not remain silent."

Whitney Young called for a domestic Marshall Plan: "They must march from the rat-infested overcrowded ghettos to decent, wholesome, unrestricted residential areas dispersed throughout our city."

Wilkins demanded pressure on the president to toughen the proposed civil rights legislation: "The president's proposals represent so moderate an approach that if any part is weakened or eliminated the remainder will be little more than sugar water."

All were competent and pertinent. But Lewis most faithfully articulated the urgency of the time. "Right away it was clear to the crowd that John Lewis did not sound like any of the other speakers they had heard," writes Drew Hansen in *The Dream*. When Lewis finished, the clapping was louder than it had been for anyone else. "On the speaker's platform every black speaker rushed up to Lewis to shake his hand and pound him on the back. Every white speaker stayed seated and stared into the distance."

◆

THOUGH THE MARCH STARTED EARLY, the speeches ran late—each one taking longer than its allotted time. D'Army Bailey, then a young activist, had hoped for more. "We were tired of the humdrum rhetoric, so we left. We were aware of how the march had been compromised," he told Euchner. "We were not in tune with being led like sheep, and we walked back to the car and drove back to the townhouse."

As the speeches rolled on, a few in the crowd fainted. It had reached 87 degrees by noon. All told, thirty-five Red Cross stations treated 1,355 people. One man died of a heart attack. There was no violence. There were only three arrests—all of them white. Later in *Esquire*, Mailer asked: "Could one dream of bringing together 200,000 whites steaming with bitterness and a hot heart of injustice on a hot summer day with no riot breaking forth?"

After much negotiation, it was decided that King's speech would come at the end. By the time he reached the podium, the sun had baked much of the energy from the day, and some, like Bailey, had already peeled off. As King edged his way toward the microphone, he said to Harry Belafonte, with a smile: "I wonder if the president will really understand what this day is all about, if he will really see its significance."

MEANWHILE, 1,150 MILES AWAY in Donaldsonville, Louisiana, residents of nearby Plaquemine had brought a small black-and-white television to the jail, where officials let Farmer watch the march in his cell. "The awesome spectacle of over 250,000 persons—black and white, Protestant, Catholic, and Jewish, young and old, northern and southern, infirm and healthy—erased all doubts as to its worthwhileness," he wrote in his autobiography.

Several years later, Farmer told me he deeply regretted not being there. "The worst decision I ever made was staying in jail during the March on Washington," he said. "I should have bailed myself out. I missed an opportunity to speak in front of a worldwide audience—TV, radio, print media. Such an opportunity had never come before and would never come again."

As King wound up his oration with the words "Thank God Almighty, we're free at last," Farmer jokingly retorted from his jail cell: "OK, Martin, give me the key. Give me the key."

Against the backdrop of the dispersing crowd, Rustin spied

Randolph alone, at the edge of the dais, taking in the scene. "I could see he was tired," he recalled, as he made his way toward his mentor and put his arm around Randolph's shoulders. "Mr. Randolph, it looks like your dream has come true," he said. "And when I looked into his eyes, tears were streaming down his cheeks. It is the one time I recall that he could not hold back his feelings."

"King's was the poetry that made the march immortal," says Horowitz. "He capped off the day perfectly. He did what everybody wanted him to do and expected him to do. But I don't think anybody predicted at the time that the speech would do what it has done since."

✦

A CAVALCADE OF LIMOUSINES came to pick up the main players and take them to the White House. With the event having mobilized so many and passed so peacefully, Kennedy was now keen to be associated with it. He had watched the march on television not long after a meeting about whether to support a coup in South Vietnam. Now, over coffee and orange juice, he posed for pictures with the leaders. They encouraged him to bolster the civil rights bill and turn his attention to disaffection among urban Black youth.

"I may suggest to you that they present almost an alarming problem because they have no faith in anybody white," Randolph told Bobby Kennedy. "They have no faith in the Negro leadership. They have no faith in God. They have no faith in government. In other words, they believe the hand of the society is against them."

The president countered with a plea for those assembled to

stress personal responsibility. "It seems to me with all the influence that all you gentlemen have in the Negro community, that we could emphasize . . . , which I think the Jewish community has done, on educating their children, on making them study, making them stay in school and all the rest."

As for the prospects regarding legislation? The party of Lincoln, explained Kennedy, had its eye on the Confederacy. "The Republicans are trying to play to the South—with some success these days." The meeting ended cordially, with Kennedy going back to discuss Vietnam with his strategists.

✦

TO THOSE WHOSE UNDERSTANDING of politics is limited to what happens in legislatures, the March on Washington achieved little. The *New York Times* observed that the demonstration "appeared to have left much of Congress untouched—physically, emotionally and politically."

In May 1964, a Gallup poll asked, "Do you think mass demonstrations by Negroes are more likely to help or more likely to hurt the Negro's cause for racial equality?" Only 16 percent of Americans— including just 10 percent of whites but 55 percent of nonwhites— said they would help.

This ambivalence was echoed within Black politics. The movement *was* divided, and those among the leadership who thought direct action and mass mobilizations were the best ways to bring an end to segregation were a minority. But the march had shown them, and the rest of the country, that those active in the struggle were not as divided and isolated as they had previously thought. This, in itself, was of enormous value. Through the march Black people got to be subjects calling for a world they wanted to live in, rather than objects opposing the world that had been imposed on them.

As such, it marked a tipping point in the progress of the movement. "The rhetoricians and the activists are correct when they say there was no major accomplishment because of the march," says onetime SNCC organizer Ivanhoe Donaldson in *Voices of Freedom*. "But at the same time, it does represent a continuum in the struggle, and the need from time to time to create exclamation points and question marks and commas, so that people can define themselves in some time frame, which is also important to an organizer to bring something to a culmination, to take people to a next step."

The march was an expression of confidence, unity, and discipline that reached beyond the South. It demanded national attention and won a global audience. "That day for a moment it almost seemed that we stood on a height and could see our inheritance," wrote James Baldwin in *No Name in the Street*; "perhaps we could make the kingdom real, perhaps the beloved community would not forever remain that dream one dreamed in agony."

3

The Speech

"WE REALLY ONLY TRUST conscious decision making," writes Malcolm Gladwell in *Blink: The Power of Thinking without Thinking.* "But there are moments, particularly in times of stress, when haste does not make waste, when our snap judgments . . . can offer a much better means of making sense of the world."

Herein lies the apparent paradox of King's delivery of the "I Have a Dream" speech. In a very real sense, King had been training for this moment his whole life. When it came, he literally set aside everything he'd prepared and went with his gut. At the time the church was to Black America what the École Normal Superieure is to France or Oxbridge is to Britain—the incubator and inculcator of a political elite. Under slavery and segregation it was one of the few places where African Americans could organize autonomously. Those who rose through its ranks were not dependent on white people for money and were among the most likely to be literate.

As one of the third generation of preachers in his family, King had always been a precocious member of the Black clergy's aristocracy. As a kindergartener he could recite biblical passages from memory. As a small child he once told his mother: "You just wait and see. I'm going to get me some big words." At fifteen he won a prize in a contest sponsored by the Black Elks, a Black fraternal organization, with a speech called "The Negro and the Constitution." As a seminary student he took homiletics: the application of the general principles of rhetoric to preaching. "Martin was a Hegelian," Jack O'Dell, who worked with King at the SCLC, told me. "He wasn't just a preacher. He was a man of the Enlightenment."

Schooled from such an early age to both lead and preach, King was part of a select corps to which Harlem Renaissance poet and intellectual James Weldon Johnson gave the name "God's Trombones." "The old-time Negro preacher of parts was above all an orator, and in good measure an actor," Johnson writes. "He knew the secret of oratory, that at bottom it is a progression of rhythmic words more than it is anything else. . . . He was a master of all the modes of eloquence. . . . His imagination was bold and unfettered. He had the power to sweep his hearers before him and so himself was often swept away. At such times his language was not prose but poetry."

Within a range of known and tested clerical structures that the preachers employed, a certain degree of improvisation was not only possible, it was expected. "They were the first of the slaves to learn to read," Johnson explains. "And their reading was confined to the Bible, and specifically to the more dramatic passages of the Old Testament. A text served mainly as a starting point and often had no relation to the development of the sermon."

✦

KING LABORED EXTENSIVELY over the text of his speech for the march. He worked on it intermittently throughout the preceding four days, fitting the writing and rewriting within a frantic schedule. He also asked two of his aides, Clarence Jones and Stanley Levison, to work on a draft. He met with key advisers on the night preceding the march to discuss what he should say the next day, and then stayed up until the early hours going over it all again.

Yet for all that careful preparation, the part of the speech that went on to enter the history books was added extemporaneously while he was standing on the steps of the Lincoln Memorial, speaking in full flight to the crowd. "I know that on the eve of his speech it was not in his mind to revisit the Dream," wrote Clarence Jones.

Euchner is not so sure. In an interview he told me that a guest in the hotel room adjacent to King's heard him rehearsing the "I have a dream" passage and that King may have not included it in the final text so as not to give away his signature finale prematurely. Moreover, he believes Mahalia Jackson's intervention may have been exaggerated. He questions whether King heard her above the cacophony of voices in that moment and, even if he did, whether he could have responded in such a manner to such a specific request.

Though including the "dream" passage was a spontaneous decision, the theme itself wasn't invented on the spot. In fact, King had been using it for well over a year. The singer and family friend Mahalia Jackson had heard him employ it at a demonstration in Detroit a few months earlier. Jackson had a particularly intimate emotional relationship with King, who would call her when he felt down for some "gospel musical therapy." "She was his favorite gospel singer," Jones told me. "And he would ask her to sing 'The Old Rugged Cross' or 'Jesus Met the Woman at the Well' down the phone." Now, standing right next to him as he was winding up his prepared text, she shouted: "Tell 'em about the dream, Martin." King never subsequently confirmed that he had heard her. But Jones says that he must have done so, because he himself had heard her and he was standing just fifteen feet away from King. Edward Kennedy, who was also standing nearby, said that he had heard her too.

King spoke some months later of the spontaneity of his decision to include the passage. "I started out reading the speech, and I read it down to a point," he said. "The audience response was wonderful that day. . . . And all of a sudden this thing came to me that . . . I'd used many times before . . . 'I have a dream.' And I just felt that I wanted to use it here. . . . I used it, and at that point I just turned aside from the manuscript altogether. I didn't come back to it."

The inclusion of the passage may have been off the cuff, but the impulse behind it was deeply informed. "When King was a student at Crozer Theological Seminary he learned several stylized sermon structures in his homiletics courses," writes Drew Hansen in *The Dream*, "such as the 'Ladder Sermon,' in which arguments are arranged in order of increasing persuasiveness, and the 'Jewel Sermon,' in which a single idea was examined from several different perspectives. . . . [There was also] the 'Rabbit in the Bushes' structure in which a preacher who feels the crowd respond should keep addressing the same idea, just as a hunter might shoot repeatedly into the bushes to see if a rabbit is there."

Throughout 1963 King made almost a speech a day. His other

commitments precluded his crafting a different address for each occasion. Instead he would weave together previously used riffs, anecdotes, and metaphors—both biblical and secular—to frame a particular argument or describe a specific situation.

"Martin could remember exact phrases from several of his unrelated speeches and discover a new way of linking them together as if they were all parts of a singular, ever-evolving speech," says Jones. "He could speak extemporaneously at all times, and while he was speaking he could be mentally cutting and pasting things he had said from other speeches. He would be mentally inserting them. Just seamlessly. That's what he did."

The task was to repurpose the range of material already available in a way that avoided reducing what was said to the platitudes of a stump speech. This would have been particularly important in 1963, when the political situation was shifting so quickly that the words that moved crowds at the beginning of the year, before Birmingham, the summer of protest, and the march, might not work at all at its end, in the wake of the tragedies of the Sunday school bombing and Kennedy's assassination.

Quite where and when King first acquired the phrase "I have a dream" is not known. Hansen traces it to a contribution at a prayer service in Sasser, Georgia, in 1962, after a church burning, or, possibly, a different service in Albany, Georgia. But Wyatt Tee Walker says he remembers King using it at least two years before the March on Washington. The first use documented by transcript is from a speech King gave on November 27, 1962, in Rocky Mount, North Carolina. Much of it precisely prefigures the version used at the March on Washington—a dream "rooted deeply in the American dream" with " little black boys and little black girls" and a meeting of "sons of former slaves and the sons of former slave-owners . . . at the table of brotherhood."

By the summer of the following year King was using the dream idiom frequently. At the Detroit rally in June, where Jackson heard it, he used it to refer to recent arson attacks: "I have a dream this afternoon, that one day, one day, men will no longer burn down houses and the church of God simply because people want to be free." He name checked some of the most prominent victims of violence. "I have a dream this afternoon that there will be a day when we will no longer face the atrocities that Emmett Till had to face or Medgar Evers had to face, but that all men can live with dignity." And he raised the issue of the exclusion of Black people from jobs and housing. "I have a dream this afternoon that one day, right here in Detroit, Negroes will be able to buy a house or rent a house anywhere that their money will carry them and they will be able to get a job."

Just a week before the march, at a huge fundraiser in Chicago for the National Insurance Association, which represented Black-owned and -operated insurance companies, he would tailor it differently. "I have a dream that one day, right down in Birmingham, Alabama, where the home of my good friend Arthur Shores was bombed just last night, white men and Negro men, white women and Negro women, will be able to walk together as brothers and sisters. I have a dream."

Clearly it was already being recognized as one of his more memorable refrains. When he finished speaking in Chicago the emcee thanked King, saying: "I don't have that eloquence, so you'll have to have another dream." Hansen points out that it even stuck in the memory of one of Bull Connor's deputies, who had been sent to inform on a meeting where King spoke in Birmingham that spring. "He said that he had a dream of seeing little Negro boys and girls walking to school with little white boys and girls," the deputy reported, "playing in the parks together and going swimming together."

"That speech was made up of a lot of elements of speeches that he had given that previous year," explains Harding. "So when I heard it I couldn't say that I was thinking the world would hold on to it the way that they did."

King' greatness as a speaker, said James Baldwin, lay "in his intimate knowledge of the people he is addressing, be they black or white, and in the forthrightness with which he speaks of those things which hurt or baffle them." .

King told his aides that the most important thing for him in any sermon was having some sense of where and how he would finish. "First I find my landing strip. It's terrible to be circling around up there without a place to land." The problem with the text that he had in hand for the day of the march was that it seemed a lot stronger on takeoff than on landing.

So the way King ended the speech (freestyling) was far more typical than the way he started it (tethered to a written text). But given the enormity of the moment, he could not simply rely on his ability to find the right words at the right time. King was an extraordinary natural orator, but even he was not so confident as to believe his best strategy on such an occasion lay in extemporizing and hoping the Spirit would find him. "This was a different audience, a different time, a different place," says Lewis. "This was truly history, and Dr. King knew it. We all knew it. We'd known it with our own speeches and he knew it with his. He was responding to the occasion. He was speaking not just to the massive audience before us, but to the president, to Congress, to the nation, to the world."

So he worked and reworked the speech, worrying away at it, determined to get it exactly right. He wanted it to be remembered like Gettysburg. He didn't want to leave anything to chance. Unfortunately for him, the politics and personalities that had so overshadowed the organization of the march complicated these aspirations. Some, through personal jealousy or political rivalry, had not wanted to concede the final speaker slot to him. They recognized that this would effectively make him the keynote speaker of the entire event. So petty were their rivalries that some in King's camp believed the only reason others agreed to his going last was because they thought that by the time he spoke, the networks would have ceased covering the march and returned to regular programming. If true, this turned out to be a major miscalculation: immediately prior to King's arrival at the podium, both ABC and NBC announced that they were interrupting their regular programming to broadcast his speech.

Only when it was pointed out that if King didn't speak last then someone would have to follow him was the matter dropped. Everyone knew he was the best speaker, and nobody wanted to take the mic in his wake. "You are wise because, the minute King has finished," Rustin told them, ". . . everybody is going to head home."

Then came the matter of timing. Rustin had allotted every speaker five minutes, with a strict warning not to exceed seven minutes. Having given King the plum slot, some were now concerned that he would dominate the proceedings by taking longer than anyone else. Wilkins threatened to cut the microphone off if King went over ten minutes. These "God's Trombones" of Johnson's were soloists by temperament, and once they got going they could be difficult to stop. Other speakers insisted that King have the same limited amount of time as everyone else.

Jones felt this was an insult to King. "With all due respect to Roy Wilkins, James Farmer, John Lewis, Walter Reuther, Rabbi so-and-so, Reverend so-and-so—with all due respect to them, these people who came, they didn't come for them," Jones told King. "They came for you."

King was upset by the determination of his allies to limit his time. "They are trying to throttle me," he said. "Maybe they're determined that I not be in a position of making a speech that will get a great response from the people."

Jones backed him up. "I don't care if they speak for five minutes—that's fine. You are going to take as much time as you need," he told him. Randolph reassured Jones that King could have as much time as he needed, with the proviso that Jones not tell the others anything about the concession. By this time, however, King had resolved that if it was what the others wanted, he would adhere to the time limit.

This would not be easy. After all, he had a lot of material to fit into the speech. "First, he had a reservoir of concepts and scriptural material from speeches he'd given elsewhere," explains Jones.

> In addition, earlier that summer before the deadline pressures were so intense, he had asked [others] for some thoughts on the tone and content of his speech. Then he and I had discussed the topics in more detail during the three weeks the King family spent at my home in Riverdale. After that, even more specifically, Martin had asked Stanley [Levison] and me to prepare a draft of the point of departure, the direction, and the substance of some of the things we thought Martin should say.
>
> It was in no way a final polished speech, but we had outlined some solid ideas. We believed the occasion was a national

extended mass meeting of our supporters. [Given this], we felt Martin had an obligation to provide leadership, offering a vision that we were involved in action, not activity; a clear-eyed assessment of the challenges we faced; and a road map of how we could best meet those challenges. Ours was a speech built around new initiatives, and Martin had expressed enthusiasm when we'd presented it to him earlier in the month.

Those who knew him well, including Jones, are keen to emphasize that King's speeches were very much his own. He would invite contributions from a range of collaborators. But the end product was always up to him and him alone. Only this time, given the importance of the occasion, he sought more input than usual. Several early versions were effectively drafted by committee. On the Saturday before the march King met with advisers at Jones's New York home. Everyone had their pet issue. Rustin wanted something about labor in it; some wanted him to use "I have a dream." Walter Fauntroy liked the "bad check" metaphor. On Monday, in Atlanta, King worked on the speech with Ed Clayton before calling him back later that night with his edits. He revised it again on the plane while flying to Washington.

On arrival in Washington, King's advisers convened in the lobby of the Willard Hotel to talk through for a final time what he was going to say. Once again, a variety of positions were advanced. "It seemed everyone had a stake in this speech, a predetermined angle," writes Jones. Ralph Abernathy said: "Martin, you have to preach. Most of the folks coming tomorrow are coming to hear you preach." Others wanted him to appeal more explicitly to the younger activists.

By now, it seems, King was feeling overwhelmed by the challenge of reconciling the wide range of inputs. "Martin looked over at me and said, 'Clarence, would you mind taking some notes?'" Jones later reported. "He suggested that when we were finished, I could organize them into something cohesive. . . . For the next few hours, I tried my best to keep track of all the information being offered up, discussed, and debated."

Around 10 o'clock King proposed that Jones take a break and return with a summary of the main points. "And yes, try to do this without too many martinis," he added wryly. Jones came back shortly after with what he thought was a faithful rendition of the discussion he had heard. He read it back to the group, and the heated debate started all over again. This was a cue for King to wrap the conversation up. "OK, brothers," he said. "Thank you so very much for your suggestions and input. I am now going upstairs to my room to counsel with my Lord."

King went to his suite and continued the redrafting. A few floors below, Walker made himself available. When King got stuck he'd call Walker, who would head upstairs as soon as he crafted something he thought would work. "When it came to my speech drafts," writes Jones, "[King] often acted like an interior designer. I would deliver four strong walls, and he would use his God-given abilities to furnish the place so it felt like home." King finished the outline around midnight and then wrote a draft in longhand.

"He was a craftsman and he spoke as a poet," recalls Andrew Young. "He used to tell me, 'You have good ideas but you don't use enough adjectives. You've got to write a little more poetically.' If you look at the copies of the speeches he wrote, he would scratch out a word five or six times, not just to get the right word but the right rhythm." This one was no exception.

After struggling with the time constraints, King decided that using both "I have a dream" and the "bad check" would make the speech too long. He discarded the former. He finished writing at 4:00 a.m. and gave the final draft to his aides to be printed and distributed to the other speakers and the press. Thanks to the extensive negotiations about what should go in to it, the final version was, unsurprisingly, both familiar and unremarkable. "The prepared speech King brought with him to the podium stayed close to standard themes from the political rhetoric of the 1960s and the oratory of the civil rights movement," writes Hansen: "the appeal to American ideals, the protest against gradualism, the call for nonviolence and racial integration within the freedom movement."

The next morning was predictably hectic. Meetings with members of Congress made the leaders late for the march, and as noted, fraught negotiations about Lewis's speech were ongoing. But in between all the other distractions King still found time to fiddle with what he'd supposedly finished the night before. When he eventually walked to the podium, the typed final version was full of cross-outs and scribbles.

"In a very real sense, the speech is truly meant to be heard," writes Jones. "And though Martin Luther King Jr. was an astoundingly talented writer, in some ways it would do him a disservice to offer the transcript of the words without the accompanying propulsive force of the voice and mind behind it. It was a performance and has always been judged as such."

✦

THE DAY AND THE EXCITEMENT had cooled a little by the time Mahalia Jackson, the "Queen of Gospel," took to the mic to sing "I've Been 'Buked and I've Been Scorned," which had been personally requested by King. When Rabbi Joachim Prinz finished his speech, the program was running half an hour behind schedule. King was sixteenth on an official program that included the national anthem, an invocation, a prayer, a tribute to women, two sets of songs, and nine other speakers. Only the benediction and the Pledge of Allegiance were to follow him. Weary from a night's travel to get there, many were anxious to make good time on the journey back and had already left. Portions of the crowd had moved off to seek respite from the heat under the trees on the Mall, while others dipped their feet in the reflecting pool. Those most eager for a view of the podium braved the sun under the shade of their umbrellas.

The area around the mic was crowded with speakers, dignitaries, and their entourages. Rustin, rarely without a cigarette hanging from his lips, shuttled back and forth making sure everything was running to plan. Wearing a black suit, black tie, and white shirt, King edged through the melee toward the podium. On his left a park ranger adjusted the microphones so they were lower. Randolph, who had just finished introducing him, was over six feet tall; King was not much more than five-six.

> I am happy to join with you today in what will go down in history as the greatest demonstration for freedom in the history of our nation.

The applause is polite. "Not everyone could hear King's words," writes Euchner in *Nobody Turn Me Around*. "The sound system, the best available, still crackled and blanked out. Far from the Lincoln Memorial people followed the words on transistor radios—and by watching the movement of bodies ahead." Those close enough hear his voice as a deep baritone—a blend of southern timbre and ecclesiastical training that was once the prevailing accent of Black politics. After the march *Newsweek* described King's voice as a church organ. But that misses one of its principal, distinctive attributes: a tremulous, quavering quality that finds its target and then hovers above it. "God's Trombones," wrote Johnson, "often possessed a voice that was a marvelous instrument, a voice [they] could modulate from a sepulchral whisper to a crashing thunder clap."

> Fivescore years ago, a great American, in whose symbolic shadow we stand today, signed the Emancipation Proclamation.

It is intriguing how in times of political polarization and crisis, in 1963 as now, Americans draw their inspiration for unity from the very president who had to wage a war in order to impose it. King starts by locating the demands of Black America as consistent with America's historical tradition rather than aberrant from it.

> This momentous decree came as a great beacon light of hope to millions of Negro slaves who had been seared in the flames of withering injustice. It came as a joyous daybreak to end the long night of their captivity.

He begins slowly, very slowly. Powerful pauses, deliberate diction, and flat, precise enunciation are hallmarks of this passage of the speech. Audiobooks run at between 150 and 160 words a minute. A slideshow presentation is usually roughly 100 words a minute. In his first minute King utters 77 words. Any concerns about time constraints he might have had previously have clearly been eclipsed by his desire to make sure that whatever he says is both heard and absorbed. By the time he's done, he'll have taken more than twice the time allotted to others.

But one hundred years later, the Negro still is not free.

So begins the first of King's many anaphoras: the rhetorical device whereby a speaker emphasizes his point by repeating a phrase at the beginning of neighboring clauses. Each time he returns to the phrase "One hundred years later," he says it just a little quicker, and by the fourth time considerably louder so that its effect is more rousing. Episodically shaking his head in a combination of disbelief and despair, with each repetition he has the chance to look up from his text and, with each return to "One hundred years later," pivot on his heels to face the crowd.

> One hundred years later, the life of the Negro is still sadly crippled by the manacles of segregation and the chains of discrimination. One hundred years later, the Negro lives on a lonely island of poverty in the midst of a vast ocean of material prosperity. One hundred years later, the Negro is still languished in the corners of American society and finds himself an exile in his own land. And so we've come here today to dramatize a shameful condition.

This is an honest and measured assessment of both the potential and limitations of what the march can achieve. It gives the movement agency: the chance to present itself, its leaders, and its agenda to the world on its own terms and articulate its demands in its own words.

In a sense we've come to our nation's capital to cash a check. When the architects of our Republic wrote the magnificent

> words of the Constitution and the Declaration of Independence
> they were signing a promissory note to which every American
> was to fall heir. This note was a promise that all men, yes, black
> men as well as white men, would be guaranteed the "unalienable
> Rights" of "Life, Liberty and the pursuit of Happiness."

This metaphor came straight from Jones, with a story that
starts in the jail cells of Alabama and ends in a New York bank vault
with one of the nation's wealthiest Republicans. Following the mass
arrests in Birmingham, the movement needed to find a large
amount of money quickly in order to pay bail for the large numbers
of young people who had been arrested. Jones, at a loss, called Harry
Belafonte for moral support. Belafonte thought he might have a solution. "I think I can stir the pot," he said. "Let me do a little leg-
work. I'll get back to you."

Belafonte called Hugh Morrow, the speechwriter for New York
Republican governor and future US vice president Nelson Rockefeller. Rockefeller had for some time been a low-profile supporter
of the civil rights movement. Morrow told Jones to come to the
headquarters of Chase Manhattan Bank in New York on the following Saturday. Jones showed up to find a security guard, a banker,
Morrow, and Rockefeller present. "Everyone would play his part,"
he wrote: "Rockefeller as the somewhat detached philanthropist,
Morrow as the careful mouthpiece, the banker as the one making
sure all the 'i's' were dotted and 't's' were crossed, the Brink's agent
with the gun making sure nothing went haywire. And me in the role
of the hat-in-hand Negro, trying hard to appear as if this were not
the strangest situation I had ever encountered."

Jones watched as more money than he'd ever seen before was
locked in a briefcase. The banker gave him a sheet of paper.

"Please sign this, Mr. Jones," he said.

"It was filigreed and stamped with official-looking seals," Jones recalled. "In bold letters along the top it read. DEMAND PROMISSORY NOTE. The banker saw the concern in my eyes. 'Banking regulations, sir. It's—required.' If I signed it, I became responsible for paying the money back. One hundred thousand dollars."

"I can't personally promise this will be paid back," Jones said.

"There are legal conditions that apply here," the banker insisted. "We need a signature or we can't release the funds."

Jones looked to Rockefeller and explained that neither he nor the SCLC could vouch for this amount of money.

"Just sign for it, Mr. Jones," said Rockefeller. "You don't need to worry about it."

Jones signed, took the money, and sent it to Birmingham, and the youngsters were released. When he was back in his Manhattan office on Tuesday, a messenger arrived and requested a signature for receipt of a letter he was carrying. Inside the envelope, stamped "Personal and Confidential," from Chase Manhattan Bank, was the promissory note he'd signed three days earlier marked PAID in red ink.

"I had seen the cash nearly bursting out of the vault of the Chase Manhattan Bank in New York," Jones recalled in a later conversation. "I knew wealth was out there, and—Mr. Rockefeller notwithstanding—I saw that most wealthy people turned a blind eye to the hungry. The same could certainly be said of the US government and its relationship to racism, uniquely positioned as it is with lawmaking and enforcing abilities. The government was rich with the power to help us and utterly miserly in doing so. They turned out empty pockets to show us there was nothing they could do. Well, we would see about that."

It is obvious today that America has defaulted on this promissory note, insofar as her citizens of color are concerned. Instead of honoring this sacred obligation, America has given the Negro people a bad check, a check which has come back marked "insufficient funds."

Those final two words, effectively the punch line, are greeted with huge cheers.

But we refuse to believe that the bank of justice is bankrupt. We refuse to believe that there are insufficient funds in the great vaults of opportunity of this nation. And so we've come to cash this check, a check that will give us upon demand the riches of freedom and the security of justice.

At this point, four minutes in and with the urging of the crowd, King starts to find his oratorical stride. From now on he will read less and speak more, redirecting his attention from the words on paper to the audience.

O'Dell, one of King's lieutenants, who stepped aside after Kennedy urged King to purge him because of his earlier membership in the Communist Party, argues that this is one of the strongest parts of the speech. "Everybody understands what a bad check is. And with that in the speech there remains an insistence that the ruling class still has to pay back—that it's not over. It's an indictment of the country that's not a dream anymore."

Some years later, O'Dell told me, he was asked to be an adviser on Ely Landau's documentary about King, in which the march features prominently, and was shocked to find that the "bad check" metaphor had been edited out. He raised its absence gently with Landau. "It's an indispensable part of the speech," he said. "I'm just wondering why it wasn't included." There was no satisfactory response. Several years later the film was screened again at a festival. O'Dell went to see it. The section still wasn't included, prompting O'Dell to reflect: "I think it's inconvenient for people to remember the speech with that section in it because it brings it up to date."

> We have also come to this hallowed spot to remind America of the fierce urgency of now.

"The fierce urgency of now" is a phrase Barack Obama would adopt during his first campaign for the Democratic presidential nomination. "I am running in this race because of what Dr. King called 'the fierce urgency of now.' Because I believe that there's such a thing as being too late, and that hour is almost upon us," he said, speaking at the Jefferson-Jackson dinner in Iowa in 2007, just a couple of months before his victory over Hillary Clinton in the caucuses there propelled him to front-runner. Given the relative timidity of his first term, when his administration rarely appeared to be acting with either ferocity or urgency, it's a reference that did not last long into his tenure. "We need the Barack Obama who ran in 2008," wrote the *Washington Post*'s Ezra Klein in 2011. "The one who believed in 'the fierce urgency of now,' rather than 'After the election, we hope.'"

> This is no time to engage in the luxury of cooling off or to take the tranquilizing drug of gradualism. Now is the time to make real the promises of democracy. Now is the time to rise from the dark and desolate valley of segregation to the sunlit path of racial justice. Now is the time to lift our nation from the quicksands of racial injustice to the solid rock of brotherhood. Now is the time to make justice a reality for all of God's children.

This is the second anaphora. It employs, with ever greater emphasis, the repetition "Now is the time." The phrase captures a reality that was particularly pertinent in 1963, when much of the civil rights leadership had been slow to acknowledge the impatience of its base. It was the lesson King had tried to convey from the Birmingham jail and that Randolph had passed on to Kennedy when he told the president: "The Negroes are already in the streets; it is very likely impossible to get them off." It is, in a sense, the lesson of every liberation campaign: a successful movement needs to recognize its most propitious moment to strike and seize it. "Sekunjalo Ke Nako," "Now Is the Time" in both Xhosa and Sotho was the campaign song of the African National Congress during South Africa's first democratic elections.

Each time King repeated "Now is the time," the crowd cheered the phrase rather than the specific imperative that followed it.

> It would be fatal for the nation to overlook the urgency of the moment. This sweltering summer of the Negro's legitimate discontent will not pass until there is an invigorating autumn of freedom and equality. Nineteen sixty-three is not an end, but a beginning. And those who hope that the Negro needed to blow off steam and will now be content will have a rude awakening if the nation returns to business as usual. [Applause.]
>
> And there will be neither rest nor tranquillity in America until the Negro is granted his citizenship rights. The whirlwinds of revolt will continue to shake the foundations of our nation until the bright day of justice emerges.

This passage, which includes words borrowed from the opening lines of Shakespeare's *Richard III*, was less a threat than a promise. Any delay in addressing the legacy of slavery, in all its manifestations, would have devastating consequences and risked widespread unrest. It was a threat made all the more real by the possibility that Malcolm X, waiting in the wings, might enter the stage from the Left.

But even though Malcolm X supported neither integration nor nonviolence, he nonetheless recognized that if nonviolent mass actions like the March on Washington were not a success, it would set back the entire antiracist struggle. The night before the march, he had visited Ossie Davis in his room at the Statler Hotel and told him: "I want you to know that if you need help on anything, I am here to help. I will be discreet. I have told the proper people that I am available. If you need to find me, I'll tell you where to reach me. If there's violence and I can help, tell me. I'll do anything."

This, Davis explained later, was part of an unarticulated but broadly understood grand strategy in which Malcolm X and the civil rights leadership colluded.

> Martin and the regular civil rights leaders were presenting to America our best face. Our nonviolent face. Our desire to be included in American society. And we wanted to show the world that we had no evil intentions against anybody. We just wanted to be included. But they also understood that America, in spite our reassurances, would be frightened and hesitant to open the doors to Black folks. So Malcolm, as the outsider, as the man they thought represented the possibilities of violence, was the counter that they could use. They would say to the powers that be, "Look, here's Martin Luther King and all these guys. We are nonviolent. Now outside the door, if you don't deal with us, is the other brother, and he ain't like us. You going to really have hell on your hands when you get to dealing with Malcolm. So it behooves you, white America, in order to escape Malcolm, to deal with us."

the highways and the hotels of the cities. We cannot be satisfied as long as the Negro's basic mobility is from a smaller ghetto to a larger one. We can never be satisfied as long as our children are stripped of their selfhood and robbed of their dignity by signs stating: "For Whites Only."

The trajectory of the speech can be understood by the progression of the anaphora deployed to this point: from "One hundred years later . . ." to "Now is the time . . ." and now "We can never be satisfied as long as . . ." Each one builds successively from past to present to future, making the argument that the legacy of slavery remains, the time to eradicate it is now, and the movement will not be stopped until the task is accomplished.

The issue of what would satisfy King was a matter of constant frustration for the Kennedy administration. In an oral history some years later, Burke Marshall remembered King as an inscrutable negotiating partner in Birmingham. "I talked to King and I asked him what he was after. He really didn't know. It was hard to negotiate with King because he had no specifics. What he wanted was something." In reality King's demand was quite clear: an end to segregation in the city. But at that time and in that place such a demand was difficult for Marshall to comprehend as credible. What King ultimately wanted was something few could imagine, and remains so today: a Birmingham free of discrimination with equal rights and opportunity for all. His demands included the end of police brutality, racial profiling, endemic poverty, and the psychic inferiority all of this brought about. The totality of these demands, at once utopian and reasonable, idealistic and just, gave the lie to the notion that King was in any way a moderate.

> We cannot be satisfied as long as a Negro in Mississippi cannot vote
> and a Negro in New York believes he has nothing for which to vote.

Here King echoes John Lewis's despair at a political culture in a moment of transition, with Democrats still the party of southern segregation and Republicans now pursuing disaffected whites in the South and the suburbs. Earlier in the day Lewis had asked: "But what political leader can stand up and say, 'My party is the party of principles'?"

> No, no, we are not satisfied, and we will not be satisfied until "justice
> rolls down like waters, and righteousness like a mighty stream."

While there have been several biblical allusions in the speech up to this point, this is the first reference taken directly from the Good Book. The quote is from Amos. One of the shepherds of Tekoa relates a vision he saw concerning Israel two years before an earthquake. Full of the wrath of the Old Testament, the Lord pledges, among other things, to punish the Israelites by sending "fire on the walls of Gaza that will consume her fortresses" and turning his "hand against Ekron till the last of the Philistines are dead." Rather than listen to the music of their harps, he vows to "let justice roll on like a river and righteousness like a never-failing stream." While one should not interpret these passages literally, one should not dismiss King's use of them as mere window dressing either. King knew the Bible well and was not careless with words. There is no shortage of more conciliatory passages he might have used. Instead he cites the cost of the United States' not satisfying demands for equality as nothing less than God's vengeance.

Now comes King's main point of departure from the prepared

text. The next section, clearly intended to wind up the speech, was supposed to be as follows:

> And so today, let us go back to our communities as members of the international association for the advancement of creative dissatisfaction. Let us go back and work with all the strength we can muster to get strong civil rights legislation in this session of Congress. Let us go down from this place to ascend other peaks of purpose. Let us descend from this mountaintop to climb other hills of hope.

King skipped this passage, for reasons about which we can only speculate. It could have been because he felt the speech was dragging or, given the response to his previous line, that he thought this section would slow it down. Certainly, from a rhetorical viewpoint, it adds little apart from the cumbersome "international association for the advancement of creative dissatisfaction"—surely a club few would ever want to join. And politically it ties the utopian vision of a postracial world to the mundane and thoroughly undeserving civil rights bill Kennedy was about to introduce to Congress. King then picked up the prepared text again.

> I am not unmindful that some of you have come here out of great trials and tribulations. Some of you have come fresh from narrow jail cells. And some of you have come from areas where your quest—quest for freedom—left you battered by the storms of persecution and staggered by the winds of police brutality. You have been the veterans of creative suffering. Continue to work with the faith that unearned suffering is redemptive.

One of the signature achievements of the civil rights movement during this era had been to transform jail time in the service of the movement from a stigma to an honor. This gave the lie to Malcolm X's taunt that the demonstration was "nothing but a church picnic." Given the thousands of people who had been arrested all over the country, it could just as easily have been called a mass gathering of former political prisoners. Indeed the scenes of comity on the Mall that day stood in vivid contrast to the vicious realities of daily life, let alone protest, elsewhere in the country.

The speech was supposed to end like this:

> With this faith we will be able to hew out of the mountain of despair a stone of hope. With this faith we will be able to transform the jangling discords of our nation into a beautiful symphony of brotherhood. Let us work and march and love and stand tall together until that day has come when we can join hands and sing, "Free at last, free at last, thank God Almighty, we are free at last."

Far worse speeches have earned their place in history. It had been delivered peerlessly, touched all the major bases, and contained some marvelous imagery. For all that, had this been the full speech, it would have done little more than summarize the same issues the other speakers had covered that day, albeit more poetically.

"As he delivered his prepared text that afternoon, I thought it was a good speech, but it was not nearly as powerful as many I had heard him make," wrote Lewis. "As he moved toward his final words, it seemed that he, too, could sense that he was falling short. He hadn't locked into that power that he so often found."

It was now that Mahalia Jackson shouted, "Tell them about the dream, Martin," arguably prompting King to continue improvising and start looking for "a place to land."

Go back to Mississippi, go back to Alabama, go back to South
Carolina, go back to Georgia, go back to Louisiana, go back to
the slums and ghettos of our northern cities, knowing that
somehow this situation can and will be changed.

Jones thought: "He's off; he's on his own now. He's inspired."
Jackson gave it another shot: "Tell them about the dream, Martin," she shouted again.

Let us not wallow in the valley of despair, I say to you today, my
friends.

The way King tells it, there was nobody else. Just him, the
crowd, and the words: a preacher and the faithful. King's wife,
Coretta Scott King, recalled, "At that moment it seemed as if the
Kingdom of God appeared. But it only lasted for a moment."

And so even though we face the difficulties of today and
tomorrow, I still have a dream.

It is a dream deeply rooted in the American dream.

"No African came in freedom to the shores of the New World,"
wrote nineteenth-century French intellectual Alexis de Tocqueville
in his landmark book *Democracy in America*. "The Negro transmits
to his descendants at birth the external mark of his ignominy. The
law can abolish servitude, but only God can obliterate its traces."
But that didn't stop them from trying. From the staging at Lincoln's
feet to King's evocation of the Constitution and Declaration of Independence, the address had been underpinned by a desire for the
Black experience to be written back into American history and embedded in its polity. Now, King wanted to carve out a place in
American mythology.

> I have a dream that one day this nation will rise up and live out
> the true meaning of its creed: "We hold these truths to be self-
> evident, that all men are created equal."

This was greeted with cheers. With the abandonment of the
text comes the removal of the final barrier between King and the
crowd, allowing him to dramatize his delivery still more effectively.
From now on, at various moments, he will raise his arms, lock eyes
with his crowd, look skyward, or shake his head. Having found comfort in the familiarity of the refrain, he looks more relaxed. It's not
so much that he's found his voice—he'd never lost it—but rather
that he's found the voice to match the occasion.

> I have a dream that one day on the red hills of Georgia, the sons
> of former slaves and the sons of former slave owners will be able
> to sit down together at the table of brotherhood.
>
> I have a dream that one day even the state of Mississippi, a state
> sweltering with the heat of injustice, sweltering with the heat of
> oppression, will be transformed into an oasis of freedom and justice.

As King reached his crescendo, writes Euchner, Ruth bat Morde-
cai sat on the Mall with children she had brought from a American
Jewish Congress group in New York, her enjoyment marred by some
Black boys horsing around. "Suddenly," she said later, "we understand.
The black boys are laughing not in mockery but in joy—at the utter
preposterousness of what Dr King promises, and at its unutterable
beauty." At that time, indeed even today, the notion of Mississippi's
being an "oasis of freedom and justice" was indeed preposterous.

> I have a dream that my four little children will one day live in a
> nation where they will not be judged by the color of their skin
> but by the content of their character.

This is the most willfully misinterpreted line in the entire speech, cavalierly abstracted by conservatives in particular to suggest that since race should not matter, racism and its legacy should not be taken into account.

> I have a dream today!

At this point the audience is hooked. He has them. He raises his right arm.

> I have a dream that one day down in Alabama, with its vicious racists, with its governor having his lips dripping with the words of "interposition" and "nullification"—one day right there in Alabama little black boys and black girls will be able to join hands with little white boys and white girls as sisters and brothers.

In *The Dream*, Drew Hansen points out that these were "references to the segregationist belief [which gained traction following the Supreme Court's *Brown v. Board of Education* decision banning segregation nine years previously] that states could refuse to obey federal orders with which they disagreed, thus 'interposing' the state governments in opposition to the federal government and 'nullifying' objectionable federal interference."

> I have a dream that one day every valley shall be exalted, and every hill and mountain shall be made low, the rough places will be made plain, and the crooked places will be made straight; "and the glory of the Lord shall be revealed, and all flesh shall see it together."

This passage is another direct biblical quote, this time from the book of Isaiah 40:4, in which a "way for the Lord" is prepared in the wilderness. The twin themes of Isaiah are judgment and salvation. With messianic zeal, the book presages the destruction that will befall Judah and Jerusalem if their inhabitants do not repent of their sins and describes the salvation that awaits them if they do.

> This is our hope, and this is the faith that I go back to the South with.

It's over. The passage for which the speech will be remembered, and which was almost not uttered, lasted just 301 words, less than a fifth of the total word count, and for two minutes and forty seconds, just over a sixth of the total time. The landing strip is now in clear view.

> With this faith, we will be able to hew out of the mountain of despair a stone of hope. With this faith, we will be able to transform the jangling discords of our nation into a beautiful symphony of brotherhood.

Here King returns to the written text for what would have been the finale. But he then departs from it again, reaching back into his repertoire for another familiar refrain, from "My Country 'Tis of Thee":

> With this faith, we will be able to work together, to pray together, to struggle together, to go to jail together, to stand up for freedom together, knowing that we will be free one day.
> This will be the day—this will be the day when all of God's children will be able to sing with new meaning:

> *My country 'tis of thee, sweet land of liberty, of thee I sing.*
> *Land where my fathers died, land of the Pilgrims' pride,*
> *From every mountainside, let freedom ring!*

And if America is to be a great nation, this must become true.

He starts with the one of the whitest states in the Union before moving on to give a panoramic vista of states going geographically from East to West and politically remaining in the North.

> And so let freedom ring from the prodigious hilltops of New Hampshire.
>> Let freedom ring from the mighty mountains of New York.
>> Let freedom ring from the heightening Alleghenies of Pennsylvania.
>> Let freedom ring from the snow-capped Rockies of Colorado.
>> Let freedom ring from the curvaceous slopes of California.

"Rustin," recalls Horowitz, "always said that King's genius was that he could simultaneously talk to a black audience about why they needed to achieve their freedom and address a white audience about why they should support that freedom. Simultaneously. It was a genius that he could do that as one Gestalt."

So now he brings the speech to a final close by drawing in the South, that part of the country struggling to find its place in the late twentieth century.

> But not only that:
>> Let freedom ring from Stone Mountain of Georgia.
>> Let freedom ring from Lookout Mountain of Tennessee.
>> Let freedom ring from every hill and molehill of Mississippi.
>> From every mountainside, let freedom ring.

The mention of each southern state receives its own cheer. King raises his right arm for several seconds and then lifts both arms so his hands, which have formed clenched fists, are level with his head.

And when this happens, when we allow freedom to ring, when we let it ring from every village and every hamlet, from every state and every city, we will be able to speed up that day when all of God's children, black men and white men, Jews and Gentiles, Protestants and Catholics, will be able to join hands and sing in the words of the old Negro spiritual:

With each "Free at last!" he raises his right arm just a little higher until it is fully extended over his head. He begins to wave farewell, even before he has finished speaking.

Free at last! Free at last!
Thank God Almighty, we are free at last!

◆

"THOUGH HE WAS EXTREMELY WELL KNOWN before he stepped up to the lectern," wrote Jones of King, "he stepped down on the other side of history."

"Many white Americans had never heard a full speech delivered by any Black person," Julian Bond told me, before joking: "We are lucky this was the first. Many probably came away thinking we were a race of incredibly gifted orators! Who knew?"

Watching the whole thing on TV in the White House, Kennedy, who'd never heard an entire King speech before, remarked: "He's damned good. Damned good." When King and some of the other speakers went to the White House immediately afterward, Kennedy greeted him with a smile and said: "I have a dream."

The speech left James Farmer crying in his Louisiana jail cell. "The conscience of the nation could not be wrung any tighter," he wrote. "I believed then, and still do, that [it] was an authentic American classic, on a par historically with Lincoln's Gettysburg Address. There are times when divine inspiration so touches a person that he rises beyond himself. In that moment, at the March on Washington, Martin Luther King was touched by a spirit that cannot be recaptured in our lifetime."

Though perhaps not quite so fulsome, most other responses to the speech praised King's achievement in giving voice to the moment. "I was not disturbed at all by its message of hope and harmony," recalled Lewis. "I have always believed there is room for both outrage and anger and optimism and love. Many, many times in my life, in many situations and circumstances, I have felt all these emotions at once. . . . Dr. King's speech, despite its lack of substance, was magical and majestic in spirit. I felt immensely inspired and moved by his affirmation of brotherhood and community. It is the spirit of his words that has stood the test of time, even in the face of the darkness and pain and division that persist in America to this day. More than anyone else that summer afternoon in 1963, he captured the spirit of hope and possibility that so many of us wanted to feel."

Almost everyone, including even King's enemies, recognized the speech's reach and resonance. William Sullivan, the FBI's assistant director for domestic intelligence, recommended, "We must mark him now, if we have not done so before, as the most dangerous Negro of the future of this nation."

The speech did a great deal for King's reputation all around. As Jones suggested, it made him a national and international celebrity "As a result of Dr. King's speech," said Mary King, a SNCC staffer, "he rose on the scene and became regarded as the major personality of the civil rights movement, and many then came to view him as Randolph had described him—the moral leader of the nation."

But if, in its immediate aftermath, the speech had any significant political impact, it was not obvious. "At the time of King's death in April 1968, his speech at the March on Washington had nearly vanished from public view," writes Hansen. "There was no reason to believe that King's speech would one day come to be seen as a defining moment for his career and for the civil rights movement as a whole. . . . King's speech at the march is almost never mentioned during the monumental debates over the Civil Rights Act of 1964 which occupy around 64,000 pages of the Congressional Record."

This was not a question of benign neglect. King's speech wasn't overlooked because it wasn't good. It was marginalized because in the last few years of his life King himself was marginalized, and few who had the power to elevate his speech to iconic status had any self-interest in doing so. His growing propensity to take on an issue like poverty, followed by his opposition to the Vietnam War, lost him the support of the political class and much of his white and more conservative base. On April 4, 1967, at the Riverside Church in New York, he delivered a speech titled "Beyond Vietnam: A Time to Break Silence."

"If we continue there will be no doubt in my mind and in the mind of the world that we have no honorable intentions in Vietnam," he said. "If we do not stop our war against the people of Vietnam immediately, the world will be left with no alternative than to see this as some horrible, clumsy, and deadly game we have decided to play."

Most who know his speeches well count the Riverside Church one as his finest. O'Dell suggests that it was his growing maturity and an ever-keener sense of his mortality that sharpened his rhetoric as he got older. "He had the Nobel Prize and he didn't know how long he was going to live," he explains. "He wasn't but thirty-nine, but he wasn't going to live much longer, and that meant he didn't have but maybe a few more speeches to give. So he had to say what he was going to say."

The nation was even less ready to hear what King had to say about America's militarism and warmongering than it was about his views on race. Andrew Young described the atmosphere following the Riverside speech: "Nationally, the reaction was like a torrent of hate and venom. This man who had been respected worldwide as a Nobel Prize winner, and as the only person in America who was advocating change without violence, suddenly applied his nonviolence ethic and practice to the realm of foreign policy. And no, [people said], it's all right for Black people to be nonviolent when they're dealing with white people, but white people don't need to be nonviolent when they're dealing with brown people. Since he was a Nobel Prize winner we expected people not to agree with it, but to disagree with certain specifics and at least to discuss it as an intelligent position that deserved at least an intelligent answer. We didn't get that. We got instead an emotional outburst attacking his right to have an opinion."

And while officialdom was keen to marginalize the messenger, Hansen chronicles how many African Americans soured to elements of the message as impatience with the enduring legacy of segregation and slavery grew and King's leverage diminished. With time the utopian element of King's speech, so crucial to its success in 1963, came to be misunderstood as naiveté. At a 1967 meeting addressed by then SNCC leader Stokely Carmichael, a seventeen-year-old woman in the audience said: "We intend to be the generation that says, Friends, we do not have a dream, we do not have a dream, we have a plan. So TV men, do not be prepared to record our actions indoors but be prepared to record our actions on the streets." Particularly ironic given that King's speech was made at a street action!

Following the riots in Watts that year, one resident said: "King, and all his talk about nonviolence, didn't mean much. Watts had respect for King, but the talk about nonviolence made us laugh.... I have a dream ... craa-ap. We don't want dreams. We want jobs."

Before the speech public opinion about King was evenly divided. Just a month after he wrote his *Letter from a Birmingham Jail*, Gallup found 37 percent of Americans had an unfavorable view of him, compared to 41 percent who were favorable. A year later, after the speech and after President Lyndon Johnson had signed the 1964 Civil Rights Act, his standing had improved slightly, 44 percent favorable, 38 percent unfavorable. In 1965, after he'd won the Nobel Peace Prize and shortly before the passage of the Voting Rights Act, his popularity dipped, with 45 percent favorable and 46 percent unfavorable. And a year later, as he began to speak out against the Vietnam War, the nation turned against him, with 33 percent viewing him favorably and 63 percent unfavorably.

For the political class King had become toxic, and his most famous speech was contaminated by association. Among the Black underclass King was still revered, but his speech was regularly misconstrued as excessively hopeful. Only after his death would the speech be resurrected and made fit for national mythology. It is important to remember that King died in Memphis supporting Black garbage workers in a battle over pay and conditions that had turned violent, a struggle centered on race and class, and in which his guiding philosophy had once again been tested and his relevance openly questioned.

"Within a few weeks of King's death the 'I Have a Dream' speech had regained all the public visibility it had lost since 1963," writes Hansen. "Newspapers and magazines reprinted lengthy sections from the speech in commemorative articles about King's career. Members of Congress—no longer skittish about publicly praising King—recalled how moved they had been when they heard King speak at the march."

It came not just to mark King's crowning moment but to define his entire political contribution.

The *Washington Post*, which did not quote the refrain the day after the march, ran an editorial in the wake of his death claiming: "The dream of which he spoke so eloquently at the Lincoln Memorial in 1963 must seem tonight, to many of his sorrowing countrymen and embittered fellow citizens, farther than ever from fulfillment. But that shining vision and bright hope will yet prevail. It must be our resolve to go forward with a greater sense of urgency to make a reality of his dream."

The day after the assassination President Johnson said: "No words of ours—and no words of mine—can fill the void of the eloquent voice that has been stilled. But this I do believe deeply: the dream of Dr. Martin Luther King, Jr., has not died with him."

Within a few weeks, notes Hansen, "a short biography called *I Have a Dream* and an unauthorized book of King quotations (also called *I Have a Dream*) had appeared for sale. *Life's* excerpts of Coretta Scott King's book about her husband were titled 'He Had a Dream.'"

The ability of America's powerful to co-opt and rebrand resistance to past inequities as evidence of the nation's essential and unique genius is as impressive as it is cynical. Such sleight-of-hand is often exercised at the same time that attempts to correct the inequalities that made such resistance necessary in the first place are ignored or marginalized. At the Republican National Convention in 2012, some of the greatest cheers were for tales of immigrants and minorities overcoming obstacles to make great personal advances, even as the party platform sought to put new obstacles in the way of upcoming minorities and immigrants.

On the day of the march itself, this process was already under way. Documentary filmmakers for the US Information Agency were hard at work on the Mall, depicting the peaceful protest as part of its Cold War propaganda. "Smile," they told the demonstrators. "This is going to Africa." Euchner quotes Michael Thelwell, a SNCC worker, as saying: "So it happened that Negro students from the South, some of whom still had unhealed bruises from the electric cattle prods which Southern police used to break up demonstrations, were recorded for the screens of the world portraying 'American Democracy at Work.'"

It was the same with the speech. Sanctified after his death, King's oration would eventually be celebrated by those who actively opposed his efforts while he lived. "Remembering King through the 'I Have a Dream' speech allowed the nation to tell itself a comforting but inaccurate story about King's legacy," writes Hansen: "King had called on America from the Lincoln Memorial to abolish Jim Crow, the nation had done so, and King had died victorious."

"The essential characteristic of a nation is that all its individuals must have many things in common," wrote the nineteenth-century French philosopher Ernest Renan, "and must have forgotten many things as well." For King's speech to be remembered in the way it has, America had to forget not just most of what was in it but also the life's work of the man who gave it, and the moment and movement that made it possible.

4

The Legacy

ON MONDAY JANUARY 21, 2013, America's first Black president was publicly inaugurated for his second term. It was a cloudy, chilly day in Washington. It also happened to be Martin Luther King Day.

Serendipity was in lockstep with ceremony and symbolism that morning. It was only the second time the two days had coincided since 1986, when America first observed King's birthday. But it was by no means the first time Barack Obama had been connected in the public imagination with King. Since Obama first emerged as a presidential hopeful, hawkers across the country had sold T-shirts with images of the two men side by side, while many commentators suggested that his election marked the culmination of King's dream.

Not only was Obama clearly aware of this association, he regularly reinforced it. As was mentioned earlier, in the run-up to his first election he had championed "the fierce urgency of now," a phrase taken straight from the dream speech. He had also called on his supporters to see the bigger picture, quoting King's promise (which was not in the speech) that "the arc of the moral universe is long but it bends toward justice." In his concession speech following his defeat in the New Hampshire primary in 2008 (which was later nominated for an Emmy after it had been set to music by will.i.am), he said: "It was the call of workers who organized; women who reached for the ballot; a president who chose the moon as our new frontier; and a King who took us to the mountaintop and pointed the way to the Promised Land." He accepted the Democratic nomination in Denver in 2008 on the forty-fifth anniversary of the dream speech—no mere coincidence in a campaign as carefully curated as his—and then failed to mention King by name—also no coincidence.

The resonance of that January morning in DC was difficult to avoid. Obama took the oath on King's Bible. Medgar Evers's widow, Myrlie Evers-Williams, read the invocation. A few days before, Clarence Jones had set about writing Obama a letter: "I'm going to ask him, 'If you could just pause during your speech on Inauguration Day and look at the Lincoln Memorial, and then in the direction of the King Memorial, and say as you are taking the oath of office, 'Martin, this one's for you.'"

The more literal the comparisons between the two men, the more likely they are to fall short. Obama stood for election and now stands at the pinnacle of American power; King never put himself before the voters, and he led a movement dedicated to challenging prevailing power. King practiced a politics that could not be accommodated within the electoral mainstream; Obama drew those who had either given up on or never practiced politics into the electoral mainstream. King was a pacifist; Obama has a kill list. They emerged not only in different ages but through different traditions, governed by different pressures and driven by different impulses. And while those traditions, one electoral, the other activist, had deep connections, they were by no means synonymous.

"The historian belongs not to the past but to the present," argues E. H. Carr in *What Is History?* "We can view the past, and achieve our understanding of the past, only through the eyes of the present. The historian is of his own age, and is bound to it by the conditions of human existence. The very words which he uses—words like democracy, empire, war, revolution—have current connotations from which he cannot divorce them."

Any contemporary discussion about the speech's legacy is inevitably informed by how we now understand the themes King raised in that moment. When a historically oppressed minority is explicitly excluded from voting, words like *race*, *equality*, *justice*, *discrimination*, and *segregation* connote something quite different from their meanings when the president is Black. King uses the word *Negro* fifteen times in the speech; in the year of its fiftieth anniversary, the term is finally being retired from the census as a racial category.

The anniversary arrives at a time of intensifying racial polarization, economic precariousness, and demographic flux that have caused acute anxiety for a sizable sector of white America. A poll conducted shortly before Obama's second inauguration found whites to be three times more likely to be pessimistic about the country's future than nonwhites. Meanwhile, for the poorest 90 percent of US families, most of whom are white, median income has been stagnant for a generation and social mobility has stalled. When respondents were asked to compare their economic class with that of their parents at the same age, a 2013 poll showed that whites were the most likely of any racial or ethnic group to say they were slipping behind, and non–college-educated whites were the only group more likely to say they had lost ground in this generation than gained it. Added to all that, non-Hispanic whites will be a minority by around 2042. In short, the privileges associated with being a white American, while considerable, are not what they used to be.

This has posed a particular challenge for the Right, which, whether embedded among southern Democrats or Republicans, has long relied on white votes and has traditionally leveraged racial animosity to its electoral advantage. During the 2012 Republican primaries, leading contenders made a barely veiled pitch for white votes with rhetoric demeaning African Americans and Latino immigrants. In Plymouth, New Hampshire (which is 96 percent white), Newt Gingrich told a crowd: "I will go to the NAACP convention and explain to the African American community why they should demand paychecks [instead of] food stamps." When it came to immigration, Mitt Romney advocated making things so tough for undocumented workers that they would "self-deport," while Joe the Plumber, the conservative darling of the 2008 presidential campaign and congressional candidate in Ohio in 2012, suggested that the country put "a fence on the damn border and start shooting."

In the absence of a class consciousness that would seek solidarity with poor people of other races, such rhetoric resonated with much of the party's overwhelmingly white base. A poll shortly before the election showed those who identified as Republican were more than twice as likely as independents to say that "Blacks supported Democrats because they were government dependents," "want something for nothing," or "are on welfare." Between 2008 and 2012 the number of Republicans who believed Obama was a Muslim, despite overwhelming evidence to the contrary, doubled; in 2010 a poll showed that about two-thirds of Republicans either believed that or were not sure whether Obama was "a racist who hates white people," and more than half believed or were not sure that he was not born in the United States and wanted the terrorists to win.

There were plenty of reasons why white voters would not have supported Obama that had nothing to do with race, and such views were by no means evenly spread among white Americans, many of whom voted for Obama; but they were nonetheless pervasive among conservatives, the vast majority of whom were white.

But the days when pandering to this base was certain to pay electoral dividends on a national scale are now gone. Since 1980, the white share of the electorate has fallen in every consecutive election bar one (1992, when Ross Perot ran). Meanwhile the Black and Latino voting blocs that the Republicans alienate with such rhetoric have been growing in strength, motivation, and organization. This made the 2012 election one of the most racially divisive in living memory. Blacks and Latinos were far more likely to vote for Obama than previous Democratic candidates, and since there were more of them than ever before, that left Republicans dependent on winning an even higher percentage of white votes than usual.

This was widely understood to be one of the key reasons for the Republican defeat in 2012, prompting a two-pronged response.

The first was to reevaluate the party's image among nonwhite Americans. This involved a substantial shift in its attitude toward immigration reform and a more cosmetic reappraisal of its rhetoric and messaging. The second was an attempt to change voter identification laws and use the courts to roll back civil rights–era legislation designed to eradicate racial discrimination in elections.

In order to pursue such a legal, political, and electoral agenda, the Right had to posit racism not only as a discrete phenomenon of the past but as one that has no discernible legacy. "There is an old disease, and that disease is cured," argued Bert Rein, the attorney challenging the validity of the Voting Right Act, which since 1965 has offered protections against racial discrimination at the polls, before the Supreme Court in 2013. "That problem," claimed Rein, "is solved." The court ruled in Rein's favor, effectively gutting one of the key provisions of the act.

With the "problem solved," white people could then be framed not as beneficiaries of racial inequality but as the victims of post–civil rights "social engineering" that, they claimed, sought to replicate the unfairness of Jim Crow. In 2009, when a white Connecticut firefighter blamed affirmative action for his failure to win promotion after he passed a qualifying test, he said: "I think we view discrimination as discrimination plain and simple. We were discriminated [against] based upon our race just like African Americans were in the past in other issues. So it's just plain discrimination." Similarly, when Jennifer Gratz was not given entrance to the University of Michigan, she sued the university, claiming that she was rejected because of affirmative action, in a case that eventually went to the Supreme Court. "They think it's OK to discriminate against some of us in order to promote diversity on their campus," she told me. "I think it's wrong. I deserved to have my application judged without my skin color playing a role, whether that role was to help or hurt me."

Such arguments are tenable only in a make-believe world where the past has no consequences and therefore no relationship to the present. "I am born with a past, and to try to cut myself off from that past . . . is to deform my present relationships," writes Alasdair MacIntyre in his book *After Virtue.* "The possession of an historical identity and the possession of a social identity coincide." The selective employment of collective identity necessary to deny this is unsustainable. Those conservatives who would say "We won the American Revolution" or "We won the Second World War" (even though they were not alive) would never say "We kept slaves" or "We segregated people"; they would claim that since they were not alive, they have no responsibility and they have not benefitted.

While the aim here is not to argue the pros and cons of affirmative action, it is worth pointing out that the primary beneficiaries of taking nonacademic criteria into account in university admissions are wealthy white people who are given beneficial treatment because they are legacies (their parents went to the same university) or the children of faculty, big donors, or the famous. "The preferences of privilege are nonpartisan," writes Daniel Golden, author of *The Price of Admission: How America's Ruling Class Buys Its Way into Elite Colleges—and Who Gets Left outside the Gates*: "They benefit the wealthy and powerful across the political and cultural spectrum, Democrats and Republicans, supporters and opponents of affirmative action, leftwing Hollywood movie stars and rightwing tycoons, old-money dynasties and nouveau riche. They ensure each fresh generation of upper-class families—regardless of intelligence or academic qualifications—access to the premier colleges whose alumni hold disproportionate sway on Wall Street and in Fortune 500 companies, the media, Congress and the judiciary."

In other words, America is not a meritocracy. Opportunities are generally apportioned on the basis of inherited privilege. And just fifty years after legal equality was granted to African Americans, that privilege is in no small part racial. The white flight from history that denies such advantages exist gained legitimacy with Obama's presidency, which gave credence to the notion that America had moved not only beyond race but racism. In the wake of his first victory, conservative commentators sought to depict his election not as a development in Black American politics but a repudiation of post–civil rights antiracism. "[Obama] is in many ways the full flowering of a strain of up-tempo, non-grievance, American-Dream-In-Color politics," writes Terence Samuel in *The American Prospect*. He continues, "His counterparts are young, Ivy League professionals, heirs to the civil-rights movement who are determined to move beyond both the mood and the methods of their forebears. . . . They've lived the dream, and represent a generation of black Americans who do not feel cut off from the larger society."

To these conservatives Obama's ascent did not just mark a new chapter in America's racial history; it shredded the entire book and then burned the remains. "Obama embodies and preaches the true and vital message that in today's America, the opportunities available to black people are unlimited if they work hard, play by the rules, and get a good education," wrote Stuart Taylor Jr. in *National Journal*. When I asked Gratz how she would tackle the legacy of segregation without affirmative action, she said: "I don't think you can look around the US and say there's institutional discrimination going on. Look at our president—the American people are by and large ready to judge people based on who they are."

Not surprisingly most civil rights organizations resisted this analysis even as they applauded Obama's election. As Ben Jealous, the head of the NAACP, told me, "We represent the National Association for the Advancement of Colored People, not a colored person." The relationship between racism, power, and representation is too complex to permit us to assume that Americans' newfound, hard-earned comfort with electing a Black president means an end to racism any more than the fact that having fathered a Black child meant the late South Carolina senator Strom Thurmond was against segregation.

Nonetheless, at the very least electorally, Obama's victory did represent a substantial development. In 1958, 53 percent of voters said they would not vote for a Black candidate for president; in 1984 it was 16 percent; by 2003 it was 6 percent. By the time Obama announced his candidacy, polling data suggested that a candidate's being over seventy-two (John McCain), a Mormon (Mitt Romney), or twice divorced (Newt Gingrich) would be a greater obstacle to being elected president than being Black. Even as Republicans alienated a sizable proportion of the Black electorate, a Black candidate, Herman Cain, was briefly a front-runner, and Condoleezza Rice received one of the most enthusiastic responses at the 2012 Republican National Convention. Republicans boast four of the country's five nonwhite governors, and more Latino senators than the Democrats. "Electoral racism"—refusing to vote for a candidate because he or she is not white—is clearly in decline. But that doesn't mean racism has disappeared, only that it has shifted focus and dissipated in some areas. Polls show, for example, that white Americans are more likely to embrace the idea of a Black man's being commander in chief than his being in a romantic relationship with a white woman.

If Obama's presidency created the opportunity for the Right to assert that African Americans had finally arrived, it sent a message to many Black Americans that they were on their way. Throughout his tenure no other bloc of voters has been more optimistic; polls during this time have consistently shown that African Americans are more likely than any other group to be bullish about their own future, believing that the country's best days are yet to come and that the economy is recovering. A Pew survey in January 2010 indicated that the percentage of Black Americans who thought Black people were better off than they had been five years earlier had almost doubled since 2007. There were also significant increases in the percentages who believed the standard-of-living gap between whites and Blacks was decreasing.

That optimism appears to be related to Obama's election. Asked in August 2011 about the effect of Obama's presidency on race relations, 48 percent of African Americans said "they had gotten a lot or a little better" as a result of his election. Asked whether race relations would improve "in the years ahead" as a result of Obama's occupancy of the White House, 64 percent of Blacks thought they would get "a lot better" or "a little better." Two-thirds believed his election had been either "the most important advance for blacks" in the past one hundred years or "one of the two or three most important."

This had been one of Obama's goals when considering whether he should run. When his wife, Michelle, asked him what he thought he could accomplish if he won, he said: "The day I take the oath of office, the world will look at us differently. And millions of kids across this country will look at themselves differently. That alone is something."

This played out in a touching episode just four months after Obama was first sworn in as president. It was May 2009, and five-year-old Jacob Philadelphia went with his family to the Oval Office for a photograph with the president because his father, a former marine, was leaving the White House staff.

Jacob and his eight-year-old brother Isaac were allowed to ask Obama one question each. The parents had no idea what they were going to say. Isaac asked why the president had gotten rid of the F-22 jet fighter. The president said it had cost too much money. Jacob declared: "I want to know if my hair is just like yours."

He was so quiet, Obama asked him to repeat the question. Jacob obliged.

Obama said: "Why don't you touch it and see for yourself?"

He bent down and lowered his head so that it was within Jacob's reach.

Jacob paused. The president prompted. "Touch it, dude!" he said.

Jacob reached out and rubbed the presidential pate.

"So, what do you think?" Obama asked.

"Yes, it does feel the same," Jacob said.

The White House photographer snapped the moment. "Every couple of weeks the White House photographers change out the photos in the West Wing," Michelle Obama said at the Congressional

Black Caucus Gala in September 2012. "Except for that one. So if you ever wonder whether change is possible, I want you think of that little Black boy in the office—the Oval Office of the White House— touching the head of the first Black president."

But while Black America's optimism has been real, the assumptions on which it is based are, in fact, mistaken. African Americans, as a group, are significantly worse off now than they were when Obama came to power. Since 2009 the gap between whites and Blacks in terms of wealth and income has increased. The overall rate of unemployment may be close to where it was when Obama took office, but Black unemployment is up by 7 percent. Meanwhile the wealth gap between Blacks and whites doubled during the most recent recession (which did not start under Obama), with the average white American now having six times more wealth than his or her Black counterpart. "It was already dismal," Darrick Hamilton, a professor at the New School in New York, told the *New York Times* regarding this disparity in wealth. "It got even worse."

So Jacob's odds of getting a decent job when he gets older have actually declined since he touched the president's hair, while the gap between his life chances and those of his white schoolmates has widened. In empirical terms, "the change that [has been] possible" for Jacob and his family under Obama has been change for the worse. It is beyond the scope of this book to argue about the degree to which Obama bears responsibility for these trends. But one cannot argue about the reality that underpins them. Far from signaling an end to racial inequality, the ascent of America's first Black president has coincided with one of the steepest descents of the economic fortunes of Black Americans since the Second World War, both in real terms and relative to whites. In short, Black Americans may feel better, but they are faring worse.

This paradox posed a particular challenge for Black politicians, who found themselves caught between the substantial needs of their constituents and the symbolic achievement of Obama's election. "If we go after the president too hard, you're going after us," Maxine Waters, a California Democrat in the House of Representatives, told a largely Black audience in Detroit in 2011.

"I have friends," Virginia state delegate Onzlee Ware from Roanoke, who is an ardent Obama supporter, told me before the 2012 election, "who say I'm a traitor if I bring up [Obama's short-comings] as an intellectual conversation."

Some, fearing a backlash, refrained from critiquing the president at all. "Too many Black intellectuals have given up the hard work of thinking carefully in public about the crisis facing Black America," said Princeton professor Eddie Glaude. "We have either become cheerleaders for President Obama or self-serving pundits."

Finally, fifty years after King delivered his speech, the geographical and racial rigidities of Black and white and North and South that framed the civil rights era have given way to something more fluid. It's true that the South remains the most conservative part of the country and the place where Black poverty and racial inequalities are most entrenched. But according to the 2010 census, of the top ten most segregated cities with a population of over 500,000, none are in the former Confederacy. Racial flashpoints, be they stop-and-frisk or school closings, are as likely, if not more so, to occur in the North than the South. Southern cities like Atlanta, Charlotte, and Houston are regularly named as the most popular by African Americans, and southern states like North Carolina and Virginia are now keenly contested in presidential elections.

With the Latino population now larger than that of African Americans, and the size of the Latino electorate soon to follow, the manner in which issues of race and ethnicity are framed is shifting. There is a long history of anti-Latino discrimination in the United States. But the roots and dynamics of that experience do not fit neatly into the narrative of slavery and segregation. Nixon's "southern strategy" of appealing to whites through thinly veiled racial messaging is today losing votes and states in the West, as its emphasis shifts from racism to xenophobia. "Republicans have really leveraged the anti-immigrant rhetoric to appeal to their white nativist base, and in the short term that might work nationally," Gabriel Sanchez, a professor at the University of New Mexico in Albuquerque and director of research for the polling organization Latino Decisions, told me. "But in the long term it will have negative effects. They are seen not as anti-immigrant but as anti-Latino."

The fastest growing racial group in the United States is Asian Americans, who now constitute 6 percent of the country's population. Adding to the churn, migration, primarily from Africa and the Caribbean, and mixed-race relationships are further complicating established racial categorizations. Obama is a prime example. As the son of a Black Kenyan immigrant and a white Kansan mother, he is not the descendant of slaves, So while he is Black, he is not African American in the original sense of that term. This caused some to question his racial authenticity when he first emerged as a public figure. And given that he is the son of an interracial couple, some do not even see him as Black. A Zogby poll conducted not long before Obama declared his candidacy revealed that 55 percent of whites and 61 percent of Latinos classified him as biracial, whereas two-thirds of Black Americans regarded him as Black. The distinction has been embraced by many since the census first started, allowing people to eschew traditional racial categories and register themselves as having more than one race.

When combined, these developments in race and geography have created a racial landscape that would have been unimaginable in 1963, not least because many of these shifts are most pronounced below the Mason-Dixon Line. Two Republican southern governors, Nikki Haley of South Carolina and Bobby Jindal of Louisiana, are of Indian descent. Of the ten states showing the steepest increase in those identifying as "more than one race," six (including Mississippi) are in the South, as are all five of the states with the sharpest rise in Latino populations.

◆

PERHAPS THE BEST WAY to understand how King's speech is seen in the context of this new and evolving racial landscape is to start with the radical transformation of attitudes toward the man who delivered it. Before his death, King was well on the way to being a pariah. As was pointed out earlier, in 1966 twice as many Americans had an unfavorable opinion of him as those who had a favorable one. *Life* magazine branded his anti–Vietnam War speech at the Riverside Church "demagogic slander" and "a script for Radio Hanoi." He died a polarizing and increasingly isolated figure. Just a week before he was assassinated, he attended a demonstration in support of striking garbage workers in Memphis. The protest turned violent, and police responded with batons and tear gas, shooting a sixteen-year-old boy dead. The press and the political class rounded on King. The *New York Times* said the events were "a powerful embarrassment" to him. A column in the *Dallas Morning News* called King "the headline-hunting high priest of nonviolent violence" whose "road show" in Memphis was "like a torchbearer sprinting into a powder-house"; the *Providence Sunday Journal* called him "reckless and irresponsible."

This was the last occasion on which King received national coverage while he was alive. Just six days after his assassination, Virginia congressman William Tuck effectively blamed him for his own murder, telling the House of Representatives that King "fomented discord and strife between the races. . . . He who sows the seed of sin shall reap and harvest a whirlwind of evil."

But in the decades since then, the mud that had been slung at him has been cleaned off and his legacy polished to the gleam befitting a national treasure. By 1999 a Gallup poll revealed that King was tied with John F. Kennedy and Albert Einstein as one of the most admired public figures among twentieth-century Americans. He was more popular than Franklin Delano Roosevelt, Pope John Paul II, and Winston Churchill; only Mother Teresa was more cherished. In 2011 a memorial to King was unveiled on the National Mall in DC, featuring a thirty-foot-high statue sited on four acres of prime cultural real estate; 91 percent of Americans (including 89 percent of whites) approved.

◆

THE PROCESS BY WHICH KING went from ignominy to icon was not simply a matter of ill feelings and painful memories eroding over time. It was the result of a protracted struggle that sheds light on how the speech for which he is best known is today understood. The bill to establish a federal holiday in his name was introduced just a few days after his death with few illusions as to its likely success, at least in the short term. "We don't want anyone to believe we hope Congress will do this," said the union leader Cleveland Robinson at a rally with King's widow in 1969. "We're just sayin', us black people in America just ain't gonna work on that day anymore." The movement gained its most popular advocate and widespread attention following the release of Stevie Wonder's hit song "Happy Birthday" in 1981, which he dedicated to the campaign. A six-million-strong petition soon followed.

Congress did eventually pass the bill, but not without a fight. In 1983 North Carolina Republican senator Jesse Helms argued: "The conclusion must be that Martin Luther King Jr. was either an irresponsible individual, careless of his own reputation and that of the civil rights movement for integrity and loyalty, or that he knowingly cooperated and sympathized with subversive and totalitarian elements under the control of a hostile foreign power." That same year, when asked if King was a Communist sympathizer, Ronald Reagan, who as president grudgingly signed the holiday into law in November 1983, said: "We'll know in thirty-five years, won't we," referring to the eventual release of FBI surveillance tapes.

This was more than simply a battle over a day: it served as a proxy for an ongoing national negotiation about how to understand the country's racial narrative. White America did not make this journey toward formal equality easily. A month before the March on Washington, 54 percent of whites thought the Kennedy administration "was pushing racial integration too fast." A few months after, 59 percent of northern whites and 78 percent of southern whites disapproved "of actions Negroes have taken to obtain civil rights." That same year 78 percent of white southern parents and 33 percent of white northern parents objected to sending their children to a school in which half the students were Black. According to Gallup, it was not until 1995 that a majority of white Americans approved of marriage between Blacks and whites.

✦

TO DISCOUNT KING—not the day dedicated to him but the man himself—would be to effectively dismiss the most prominent and popular proponent of civil rights. That in turn would demand some other explanation for how America shed the stigma of segregation and came to imagine itself as a modern, nonracial democracy. For while the means by which codified segregation came to an end— mass marches, civil disobedience, and grassroots activism—was not consensual, the country did eventually reach agreement that it had to end. But there is no plausible account of how American society got from Rosa Parks to Michael Jackson, let alone Barack Obama, that does not place King front and center.

"America was like a dysfunctional drug addict or alcoholic that was dependent on racial segregation," says Jones. "It had tried other treatments and failed. Then comes along Martin Luther King with his multistep program—recovery, nonviolence, civil disobedience, and integration—and forces America to publicly confront its conscience. So that its conscience would collectively see as a nation the contradiction between the way it treated 12 percent of its population who are dark-skinned and the precepts and principles enshrined in our Declaration of Independence. And that recovery program enabled America to embark on the greatest political transformation in history."

So white America came to embrace King in the same way that most white South Africans came to accept Nelson Mandela—grudgingly and gratefully, retrospectively, selectively, without grace but with considerable guile. By the time they realized that their dislike of him was spent and futile, he had created a world in which admiring him was in their own self-interest. Because, in short, they had no choice.

The only question remaining was what version of King should be honored. To remember him as a leader who sought greater government intervention to help the poor and branded the United States "the greatest purveyor of violence in the world today" would sacrifice posterity for accuracy. He did stand for those things. But those issues, particularly at a time of war and economic crisis, remain live, divisive, and urgent. To associate him with them would not raise him above the fray but insert him into it, leaving him as controversial in death as in life.

Remembering him, on the other hand, as the man who spoke eloquently and forcefully against codified segregation presents him as a unifying figure whose principled stand rescued the nation in a moment of crisis. "Our country has chosen what they consider to be the easier way to work with King," says Harding, who drafted King's speech against the Vietnam War. "They are aware that something very powerful was connected to him and he was connected to it. But they are not ready to really take on the kind of issues he was raising even there."

"I Have a Dream" did not just emerge as King's most famous speech, it became as inextricably connected with its speaker as the Little Red Book did with Mao or $E=mc^2$ did with Einstein. The King whom America wanted to commemorate, to the exclusion of all others, was the visionary who spoke of his dream under Lincoln's shadow.

This was not achieved by fiat. No nefarious mind or secret committee plotted to lull the nation into preserving King in the collective memory in this fashion. But it did not happen by accident either. This was where the battle over whether and how to remember him had settled. For liberals and civil rights activists, there was logic in the memory of King being tied to the day when his oratorical force was introduced to the world, the civil rights movement came together for the biggest demonstration in the capital's history, and, in Baldwin's words, Black America "stood on a height."

"The business of wrapping our arms around 'I Have a Dream' while we blind ourselves to the kind of work that's necessary for the creation of dreams to be manifest is simply a part of so much of what is our nature as humans and Americans," continues Harding. "We want to get the most for the least effort and energy."

Recalling King and the speech in this manner was logical, even if it was partial, because enough people had a stake in remembering the speech to make each version plausible. But that doesn't make it any less problematic. A framing of this sort not only undermines King's legacy but tells an inaccurate story about the speech itself.

King made explicit reference in his oration to both the limits of legal remedy and the need for economic redress to confront the consequences of centuries of second-class citizenship. "One hundred years later, the life of the Negro is still sadly crippled by the manacles of segregation and the chains of discrimination," he says. "One hundred years later, the Negro lives on a lonely island of poverty in the midst of a vast ocean of material prosperity." Later he goes on to insist: "We refuse to believe that there are insufficient funds in the great vaults of opportunity of this nation." No reasonable reading of this can limit King's vision to just doing away with Jim Crow. Only by willfully conflating codified segregation and racism, and ignoring not just what King had said elsewhere but also the ample contrary evidence in the speech, could one claim he was arguing that the answer to America's racial problems lay in merely changing the law.

As the radical academic Angela Davis points out with reference to slavery, ending bad laws may be a precursor to emancipation, but it is by no means a guarantee. "There was the negative abolition of slavery—the breaking of chains—but freedom is much more than just the abolition of slavery," she told me. "What would it have meant to provide economic security to everyone who had been enslaved, to have brought about their participation in governance and politics and access to education? That didn't happen. We are still confronted by the failure of the affirmative side of abolition all these years later."

When it comes to assessing the political content of the speech, the distinction between segregation and racism is crucial. To the extent that King's words were about bringing an end to codified legal segregation, the dream has been realized. The signs have been taken down, the laws have been struck from the book. Since 1979 Birmingham, Alabama, has had only Black mayors. If simply being Black, as opposed to the historical legacy of racism, was ever the sole barrier to economic, social, or political advancement, that obstacle has been officially removed.

But to the extent that the speech was about ending racism, one can say with equal confidence that its realization is not even close. Black unemployment is almost double that of whites, Black child poverty is almost triple that of whites. Black male life expectancy in Washington, DC, is lower than male life expectancy in the Gaza Strip. One in three Black boys born in 2001 stands a lifetime risk of going to prison; more Black men were disenfranchised in 2004 because they were felons than in 1870, the year the Fifteenth Amendment ostensibly guaranteed the Black male franchise.

Bayard Rustin pointed this out as early as 1965 in his aforementioned essay in *Commentary*. "The very decade which has witnessed the decline of legal Jim Crow has also seen the rise of *de facto* segregation in our most fundamental socio-economic institutions," he wrote. "More Negroes are unemployed today than in 1954, and the unemployment gap between the races is wider.... Legal niceties aside, a resident of a racial ghetto lives in segregated housing, and more Negroes fall into this category than ever before."

The speech was clearly more about wider racism than about just legal segregation. The motivation behind insisting otherwise is integrally tied to the comfort that doing so brings. By fudging the distinction between racism and segregation, or actively misinterpreting them, it is possible to cast racism as an aberration of the past. Only then can the vast differences in the material positions of

Blacks and whites be understood as the failings of individuals rather than the consequences of ongoing institutional, economic, and political exclusion. And only then does an emphasis on the single line of the speech that says "they will not be judged by the color of their skin but by the content of their character" make any sense.

The misreading is most glaring today in discussions of affirmative action. King was a strong proponent of taking race and ethnicity into account in job appointments and college admissions, in order to redress historical imbalances. "It is impossible to create a formula for the future," he wrote, "which does not take into account that our society has been doing something special against the Negro for hundreds of years."

Yet the Right has come to rely on the "content of their character" line in the speech to use King as an antiracist cover for their opposition to affirmative action. In 1986 Reagan said: "We are committed to a society in which all men and women have equal opportunities to succeed, and so we oppose the use of quotas. We want a colorblind society, a society that, in the words of Dr. King, judges people not on 'the color of their skin but by the content of their character.'" Hansen points out that ads supporting California's Proposition 209, doing away with affirmative action, featured King delivering that line alone and then the words: "Martin Luther King was right. . . . Let's get rid of all discrimination."

Such distortions in turn explain the ambivalence voiced by a significant element of the Black intelligentsia and antiracist activists more generally when discussing "I Have a Dream." It's not the speech itself about which they are reticent but rather the way King has been co-opted and his message corrupted. King's elevation to a patriotic mascot praising America's relentless and inevitable progress to better days often rankles. "There's a danger of only seeing him as a dreamer," Cheryl Sanders, a Howard University School of Divinity professor, has argued. "If we only see him as a dreamer, we too easily let ourselves off the hook from dealing with the realities that he was dealing with."

The conservative rendition, in which King ostensibly claims that racism is tackled not by challenging inequalities but ignoring them, is infuriating. "Tragically, King's American dream has been seized and distorted by a group of conservative citizens whose forebears and ideology have trampled King's legacy," writes Georgetown professor Michael Eric Dyson in *I May Not Get There with You*. "If King's hope for radical social change is to survive, we must wrest his complex meaning from [the conservatives'] harmful embrace. If we are to combat the conservative misappropriation of King's words, we must first understand just how important—and problematic—King's speech has been to American understandings of race for the past thirty years."

Despite the misreading of it, Dyson is profoundly appreciative of the speech. "'I Have a Dream' is unquestionably one of the defining moments in American civic rhetoric," he argues. "Its features remain remarkable: The eloquence and beauty of its metaphors. The awe-inspiring reach of its civic ideals. Its edifying call for spiritual and moral renewal. Its appeal to transracial social harmony. Its graceful embrace of militancy and moderation. Its soaring expectations of charity and justice. Its inviolable belief in the essential goodness of our countrymen. These themes and much more came out that day."

But he goes on to make a passionate, if somewhat regretful, plea for a decade-long moratorium on listening to or reading the speech, in the hope that Americans might take stock of their contemporary political responsibilities and seek out a fuller appreciation of King's contributions. "We have been ambushed by bizarre and sophisticated distortions of King's true meaning," he writes. "If we are to recover the authentic purposes of King's address, we must dig beneath his words into our own social and moral habits."

The trouble is that when it comes to divining what "the authentic purposes of King's address" are, there is substantial disagreement. Ironically, given that the theme of the speech was racial unity, those differences are most pronounced in terms of race. According to a Gallup poll in August 2011, the month the King monument was unveiled in Washington, most Blacks believed both that the government has a major role to play "in trying to improve the social and economic position of blacks and other minority groups" and that new civil rights laws are needed "to reduce discrimination against blacks." The figures for whites on the same issues were 19 and 15 percent, respectively. Conversely, over half of whites believed civil rights for Blacks had "greatly improved" in their lifetime, compared to just 29 percent of Blacks.

Whites were almost six times more likely than Blacks to believe that Obama's policies would "go too far in promoting efforts to aid the black community," while Blacks were twice as likely to believe that they would not go far enough. Other polls show that whites are four times as likely to believe that America has achieved racial equality and less than half as likely to believe the country will never achieve it, while blacks are four times more likely to believe "racism against blacks among police officers" is very common.

In short, Black and white Americans have very different lived experiences. I've insisted throughout on qualifying the segregation that has been eliminated as being either "codified" or "legal," for the simple reason that while the de jure enforcement of segregation has been banned, the de facto reality of it remains prevalent. Any journey through an American city, where undeclared and widely recognized geographical boundaries separate the races and their life chances, will bear this out. Blacks and whites are less likely to see the same problems, and they're more likely to disagree on the root causes of those problems and, therefore, unlikely to agree on a remedy. "For those who concentrate so much on that one line about 'the color of their skin' and 'the content of their character,'" says Harding, "I wonder how, with the resegregation of our schools and communities, do you get to know the content of anyone's character if you're not willing to engage in life together with them."

While Blacks and whites broadly concur that things have improved in the last half century, there is precious little common ground on either how far they've come or how far they have to go. "Whatever the civil rights movement did or did not accomplish, there remain very different perspectives, on average, between blacks and whites on how they view the country," Vincent Hutchings, a political scientist at the University of Michigan who studies racial politics, told *USA Today*.

Incredibly, there is pretty much only one question on which the views of Black and white Americans do coincide, which is whether they believe King's dream has been realized. Whenever that question has been asked by major pollsters in various ways over the past seven years, the discrepancy between the responses of Blacks and whites rarely topped double figures. If they agree about the extent to which the problems raised in the speech have been solved, but disagree on what those problems are and how close they are to a solution, one can only conclude that even as they listen to the same speech, they hear very different things.

If there is a weakness in the speech, it is this. While Wyatt Walker was wrong to describe the "I Have a Dream" sequence as "trite" and "clichéd," it is nonetheless true that, taken as a whole, the speech is sufficiently nebulous in its demands and broad in its scope that it opens itself up to interpretations that are not only varied but arguably contradictory.

Many of the images King evokes in his dream sequence are simple: "little black boys and little black girls [joining] hands with little white boys and little white girls" and "the sons of former slaves and the sons of former slave owners . . . [sitting] down together at the table of brotherhood." Meanwhile, descriptions of the means by which we might reach that Promised Land are intermittent and often vague: "Go back to Georgia, go back to Louisiana, go back to the slums and ghettos of our northern cities, knowing that somehow this situation can and will be changed."

To the extent that the American dream is about equal opportunity and social mobility, one could claim that the dream King evokes is "deeply rooted" in it. It speaks to the hope that African Americans will one day be able to share the same aspiration as other Americans. But to the extent that the American dream is about arriving in the New World and being able to reinvent yourself by casting off the repressive shackles of the Old, that dream will always be beyond African Americans, precisely because of the conditions under which their ancestors came to America as slaves. Of the many ways in which a person may reinvent herself or himself, replacing a legacy of forced capture, enslavement, and discrimination with one of free and purposeful migration and full citizenship is not among them.

So while claiming that the speech is limited to calling for an end to segregation is a stretch, it is not surprising that some understand the vision laid out in it in simplistic terms.

"Has King's dream been realized?" is, to my mind, one of the two most common and least interesting questions asked about the speech. The other is "Does Obama represent the fulfillment of King's dream?" The short answer to both is a clear no. The longer answer, however, is far more interesting than the questions deserve.

We know that King's dream was not limited to the rhetoric of just one speech. To judge a life as full and complex as his by one fifteen-minute address, some of which was delivered extemporaneously, is neither respectful nor serious. "As things stand, 'I Have a Dream' has been identified as King's definitive statement on race," explains Dyson. "To that degree it has become an enemy to his moral complexity. It alienates the social vision King expressed in his last four years. The overvaluing and misreading of 'I Have a Dream' has skillfully silenced a huge dimension of King's prophetic ministry."

It is implausible to imagine that were King to be raised from the dead, he would look at America's jails, unemployment lines, soup kitchens, and inner-city schools and think his life's work had been accomplished. Whether one believes that these inequalities were caused by individuals' making bad choices or by institutional discrimination, it would be absurd to claim that such a world bears any resemblance to the one King set out to create.

Nor is there anything to suggest that this view would have been much altered by the presence of a Black man in the White House.

The aim of the civil rights movement was equality for all, not the elevation of one. So while it's a reasonable guess that King, like most Black Americans, would have been delighted by Obama's victory, it's unlikely he would have claimed that victory as his own, even if it was in no small part a product of his struggle.

For all that, there is a literal and unsatisfactory, but nonetheless revealing, answer to the question "Has King's dream has been realized?" This answer resides in the speech itself:

> We can never be satisfied as long as the Negro is the victim of the unspeakable horrors of police brutality. We can never be satisfied as long as our bodies, heavy with the fatigue of travel, cannot gain lodging in the motels of the highways and the hotels of the cities. We cannot be satisfied as long as the Negro's basic mobility is from a smaller ghetto to a larger one. We can never be satisfied as long as our children are stripped of their selfhood and robbed of their dignity by signs stating: "For Whites Only." We cannot be satisfied as long as a Negro in Mississippi cannot vote and a Negro in New York believes he has nothing for which to vote. No, no, we are not satisfied, and we will not be satisfied until "justice rolls down like waters, and righteousness like a mighty stream."

Let's, for the sake of argument, posit that these are the only conditions spelled out in the speech, which they are not, and the only benchmarks King ever set out, which they are not. We have here five concrete demands and one that is rhetorical. Two, one could argue, are limited to segregation and have been met. With all exceptions granted for individual cases of discrimination, Black Americans can stay in any motel they please, and "For Whites Only" signs no longer exist. According to CNN exit polls, meanwhile,

Black voters, who make up 37 percent of Mississippi, constituted 33 percent of the electorate there in 2008 and 36 in 2012. In New York the same polls showed 100 percent of Black voters backed Obama in 2008 and 94 percent in 2012. So Black people can vote in Mississippi, and, as far as such percentages imply motivation, they feel they have something to vote for in New York. So far so good.

When it comes to "police brutality," however, it's difficult to imagine that King would derive much satisfaction from the current situation. Black Americans, particularly men, are by far the most likely of any racial group to die in police custody, to be executed, or to be stopped, searched, jailed, or given long sentences. According to the New York Civil Liberties Union there have been five million stop-and-frisks in New York alone in the past decade, mostly of Black and Hispanic men. The New York Police Department has admitted that almost nine out of ten of those affected were completely innocent of any violation, let alone a crime. In a hearing on the issue n Manhattan federal court, State Senator Eric Adams explained how New York Police Commissioner Ray Kelly told him of his policy of terrorizing Black and Latino neighborhoods: "[Kelly] stated that he targeted and focused on [Blacks and Latinos] because he wanted to instill fear in them that every time they left their homes they could be targeted by police."

When it comes to the mobility of Black people being restricted to smaller and larger ghettos, the latest census as of this writing shows that just over a third of Black Americans live in areas where poverty is below the national average, as opposed to two-thirds of whites and 40 percent of Latinos. Just over 10 percent live in areas where the poverty rate is roughly three times the national average, and another 36 percent also live in areas of high poverty. In other words, if there is any mobility at all in this regard, large numbers of Black people have not moved very far.

Each reader will have his or her own opinion on the degree to which this entire picture amounts to a vision of justice and righteousness flowing freely: it is mine that King would be far from satisfied. The value of tallying his rhetoric in such terms, as though one could assess the relevance of the speech and perspicacity of its imagination in terms of data, is limiting in the extreme. But it does serve to illustrate that even when tailored narrowly, the answer is no less categorical.

The claim that Obama's election has some connection to King's legacy has some substance. As Obama himself has often conceded, his election would not have been possible without the civil rights movement, which created the conditions for the arrival of a new generation of Black politicians. Not only did the movement make it possible for African Americans to vote in the large numbers that would help Obama win in southern states like Florida, North Carolina, and Virginia, but it was also responsible for the affirmative action that would get them into college and help them land the kinds of jobs in both the public and private sectors from which America draws much of its political class.

Less than a month after Obama declared his candidacy in 2007, he gave a speech at Brown African Methodist Episcopal Chapel in Selma, Alabama, a key organizing center during the civil rights era. "I'm here because somebody marched," he said. Citing the biblical tale of Joshua's succession to Moses, he continued, "I'm here because you all sacrificed for me. I stand on the shoulders of giants. I thank the Moses generation; but we've got to remember, now, that Joshua still had a job to do."

That job, as he saw it, was not to protest but to govern. "The civil rights generation saw politics as the next step in the struggle for civil rights," says Salim Muwakkil, an editor for the political monthly *In These Times*. "Their aim was to get their agenda taken up by whoever won. But this new generation do not conceive politics as the next step, but just as what it is—politics. Their aim is to win."

The symbolic nature of those victories, when they happen, is clear. America's election of a Black president was understood around the world as a significant event in its own right. On that election night, people danced in the streets of Harlem, and policemen on the South Side of Chicago shouted his name from their patrol cars. "I celebrated his victory," explains left-wing Uruguayan writer Eduardo Galeano, who is nevertheless critical of Obama's foreign policy. "This is a country with a fresh tradition of racism. In 1942 the Pentagon sent an order preventing the transfusion of Black blood to white soldiers. In history seventy years is nothing. It's just a moment. So in a country like this the victory of Obama was worth celebrating."

The question still remains, however, of the degree to which that victory has any impact on African Americans. As we have seen, African Americans are no better off materially as a result of his election, even if they may have been worse off had he lost. While symbols should not be dismissed as insubstantial, they should not be mistaken for substance either. The presence of underrepresented people in leadership positions has any significantly positive meaning, beyond their own personal advancement, only if it challenges whatever obstacles created the conditions for that underrepresentation. To believe otherwise is to trade equal opportunities for photo opportunities, whereby a system looks different but acts the same.

"The Republican administration is the most diverse in history," explained Angela Davis as Obama's primary campaign for his first term gained traction. "But when the inclusion of Black people in the machine of oppression is designed to make that machine work more efficiently, then it does not represent progress at all. We have more Black people in more visible and powerful positions. But then we have far more Black people who have been pushed down to the bottom of the ladder. When people call for diversity and link it to justice and equality, that's fine. But there's a model of diversity as the difference that makes no difference, the change that brings about no change."

The point here is not that Obama's victories did not make any difference; given the agenda of his Republican opponents, they clearly did. Rather, it is that his election does not, in and of itself, represent the kind of change that King either referred to in his speech or advocated generally. Obama's rise during a period when Black America has been in economic decline illustrates not the advance of the Black community but its growing stratification. As Arundhati Roy explained in her essay "Do Turkeys Enjoy Thanksgiving?": "A few carefully bred turkeys—the occasional Colin Powell or Condoleezza Rice—are given absolution and a pass to Frying Pan Park. The remaining millions lose their jobs, are evicted from their homes, have their water and electricity connections cut, and die of AIDS. Basically they're for the pot. . . . Who can say that turkeys are against Thanksgiving? They participate in it!"

One may argue about the degree to which, on the domestic front, Obama has attempted to shift the balance in the direction King would have endorsed. But given that King stepped up his campaigning for the poor at the very point when President Johnson was launching his War on Poverty and creating the Great Society, it is unlikely that King would have found the pace and scale of Obama's reforms sufficient.

Meanwhile, the views of King and Obama on foreign policy are quite different. In King's acceptance of the Nobel Prize in 1964, he said: "Violence never brings permanent peace. It solves no social problem: it merely creates new and more complicated ones." When Obama accepted his own Nobel Prize in 2009, he insisted: "There will be times when nations—acting individually or in concert—will find the use of force not only necessary but morally justified." Obama went on to distinguish himself from King and Mahatma Gandhi in terms of the different roles they played within the polity.

> I make this statement mindful of what Martin Luther King Jr. said in this same ceremony years ago. . . . But as a head of state sworn to protect and defend my nation, I cannot be guided by their examples alone. I face the world as it is, and cannot stand idle in the face of threats to the American people. For make no mistake: Evil does exist in the world. A nonviolent movement could not have halted Hitler's armies. Negotiations cannot convince al Qaeda's leaders to lay down their arms. To say that force may sometimes be necessary is not a call to cynicism—it is a recognition of history, the imperfections of man, and the limits of reason.

King dreamed of dismantling the machinery of international violence, not giving Black people an equal opportunity to operate and refine it.

✦

IN THE FINAL ANALYSIS, to ask whether King's dream has been realized is to misunderstand both his overall politics and the specific ambition of his speech. King was not the kind of activist who pursued a merely finite agenda. The speech in general and the dream sequence in particular are utopian. Standing in the midst of a nightmare, King dreams of a better world where historical wrongs have been righted and good prevails. That is why the speech means so much to me and why I believe that, overall, it has stood the test of time.

I was raised in Britain during the Thatcher years, a time when idealism was mocked and "realism" became an excuse for capitulation to the "inevitability" of unbridled market forces and military aggression. To oppose that agenda was regarded, by some on the Left as well as the Right, as impractical and unrealistic. Realism has no time for dreamers. Realism comes with the adjectives *hard-headed*, *unpalatable*, and *harsh*. If some are to be believed, realism not only sets out the parameters of our politics but also defines their outcome. When they say "Face up to political reality" they really mean "Accept political destiny." While it is true that we cannot live on dreams alone, the absence of utopian ideas leaves us without a clear ideological and moral center and therefore facing a void in which politics is deprived of any liberatory potential and reduced to only what is feasible in any given moment.

With a civil rights bill pending and the white population skittish, King could have limited his address to what was immediately achievable. He might have spelled out a ten-point plan and laid out his case for tougher legislation or made the case for fresh campaigns of civil disobedience in the North. He could have reduced himself to an appeal for what was possible in a time when what was possible and pragmatic was neither satisfactory nor sustainable.

Instead he swung for the bleachers. Not knowing whether the task of building the world he was describing was Sisyphean or merely Herculean, he called out in the political wilderness, hoping his voice would someday be heard by those with power to act upon it. In so doing he showed that it is not naive to believe that what is not possible in the foreseeable future may nonetheless be necessary, worth fighting for, and worth articulating. The idealism that underpins his dream is the rock on which our modern rights are built and the flesh on which pragmatic parasites feed. If nobody dreamed of a better world, what would there be to wake up to?

Bibliography

Anderson, Jervis. *A. Philip Randolph: A Biographical Portrait.* Berkeley: University of California Press, 1972.

Angelou, Maya. *All God's Children Need Traveling Shoes.* London: Virago, 1987.

Branch, Taylor. *Parting the Waters: America in the King Years, 1954–63.* New York: Simon & Schuster, 1988.

Brinkley, Douglas. *Mine Eyes Have Seen the Glory: The Life of Rosa Parks.* London: Weidenfeld and Nicolson, 2000.

Carr, Edward Hallett. *What Is History? The George Macauley Trevelyan Lectures Delivered in the University of Cambridge, January–March 1961.* London: Penguin, 1990.

Cash, Wilbur Joseph. *The Mind of the South.* New York: Vintage, 1991.

Clayborne, Carson, et al. *The Eyes on the Prize Civil Rights Reader: Documents, Speeches and Firsthand Accounts from the Black Freedom Struggle, 1954–1990.* New York: Penguin, 1991.

Bryant, Nick. *The Bystander: John F. Kennedy and the Struggle for Black Equality.* New York: Basic Books, 2006.

D'Emilio, John. *Lost Prophet: The Life and Times of Bayard Rustin.* Chicago: University of Chicago Press, 2003.

Dyson, Michael Eric. *I May Not Get There with You: The True Martin Luther King Jr.* New York: Free Press, 2001.

Euchner, Charles. *Nobody Turn Me Around: A People's History of the 1963 March on Washington.* Boston: Beacon, 2010.

Farmer, James. *Lay Bare the Heart: An Autobiography of the Civil Rights Movement.* New York: Plume, 1986.

Frady, Marshall. *Martin Luther King, Jr.* New York: Viking, 2002.

——. *Wallace: The Classic Portrait of Alabama Governor George Wallace.* New York Random House, 1968.

Gladwell, Malcolm. *Blink: The Power of Thinking without Thinking.* New York: Little Brown, 2005.

Hampton, Henry, and Steve Fayer. *Voices of Freedom: An Oral History of the Civil Rights Movement from the 1950s through the 1980s.* New York: Bantam Books, 1991.

Hansen, Drew D. *The Dream: Martin Luther King, Jr., and the Speech That Inspired a Nation.* New York: HarperCollins, 2003.

Honey, Michaek K. *Going down Jericho Road: The Memphis Strike, Martin Luther King's Last Campaign.* New York: W. W. Norton, 2007.

Johnson, James Weldon. *God's Trombones: Seven Negro Sermons in Verse.* New York: Penguin, 2008.

Jones, Clarence B., and Stuart Connelly. *Behind the Dream: The Making of the Speech That Transformed a Nation.* New York: Palgrave, 2010.

Kapuscinski, Ryszard. *Shah of Shahs.* New York: Vintage, 1992.

Lewis, John, with Michael D'Orso. *Walking with the Wind: A Memoir of the Movement.* New York: Simon & Schuster, 1998.

Marable, Manning. *Malcolm X: A Life of Reinvention.* New York: Viking, 2011.

Marqusee, Mike. *Redemption Song: Muhammad Ali and the Spirit of the Sixties.* London: Verso, 2000.

Marx, Karl. *The Eighteenth Brumaire of Louis Bonaparte.* Peking: Foreign Language Press, 1978.

Moody, Anne. *Coming of Age in Mississippi: The Classic Autobiography of Growing Up Poor and Black in the Rural South.* New York: Laurel, 1968.

Raines, Howell. *My Soul Is Rested: The Story of the Civil Rights Movement in the Deep South.* New York: Penguin, 1977.

Remnick, David. *The Bridge: The Life and Rise of Barack Obama.* New York: Vintage Books, 2010.

Roberts, Gene, and Hank Klibanoff. *The Race Beat: The Press, the Civil Rights Struggle and the Awakening of a Nation.* New York: Vintage, 2006.

Robin, Corey. *The Reactionary Mind: Conservatism from Edmund Burke to Sarah Palin.* New York: Oxford University Press, 2010.

Williams, Juan. *Eyes on the Prize: America's Civil Rights Years, 1954–65.* New York: Penguin, 1987.

Index

About Haymarket Books

Haymarket Books is a nonprofit, progressive book distributor and publisher, a project of the Center for Economic Research and Social Change. We believe that activists need to take ideas, history, and politics into the many struggles for social justice today. Learning the lessons of past victories, as well as defeats, can arm a new generation of fighters for a better world. As Karl Marx said, "The philosophers have merely interpreted the world; the point, however, is to change it."

We take inspiration and courage from our namesakes, the Haymarket Martyrs, who gave their lives fighting for a better world. Their 1886 struggle for the eight-hour day reminds workers around the world that ordinary people can organize and struggle for their own liberation.

For more information and to shop our complete catalog of titles, visit us online at www.haymarketbooks.org.

Also from Haymarket Books

I Am Troy Davis
Jen Marlowe and Martina Davis-Correia with Troy Anthony Davis

The John Carlos Story
Dr. John Carlos with Dave Zirin

Black Power Mixtape
Edited by Göran Olsson, with contributions by Angela Davis
and Stokely Carmichael